APPLE WATCH SERIES 9 USER GUIDE

A Complete Step By Step Manual for Beginners and Seniors on How To Navigate Through The New Apple Watch Series 9 With Tips & Tricks For WatchOS

BY

TONY D. FOGG

Copyright © 2024 TONY D. FOGG

All rights reserved. No part of this book shall be reproduced, stored in a retrieval system, or transmitted by any means, electronic, mechanical, photocopying, recording, or otherwise, without written permission from the publisher. Although every precaution has been taken in the preparation of this book, the publisher and author assume no responsibility for errors or omissions. Nor is any liability assumed for damages resulting from the use of the information contained herein.

Note: The author has made all efforts to ensure the information in this publication is accurate, however this book should be considered unofficial as it's not endorsed by Apple Inc.

Table of Contents

INTRODUCTION 1

FEATURES OF APPLE WATCH SERIES 9 2

   Design 2

   Durability 3

   Double Tap Gesture 4

   Battery 5

   Storage space 5

SET UP YOUR APPLE WATCH 6

APPLE WATCH BAND 14

   How to wear your Watch Band 14

   Change your watch band 15

GET STARTED 20

   Apple Watch Series 9 20

   Basic gestures 21

   Use the Double-Tap feature to perform actions on your watch 21

   The Apple Watch application 22

   Charge your Watch 24

      Setup your charger 24

      Start charging your Watch 25

      See the power remaining 26

Save battery power 26

Switch back to normal power mode 28

Check when last you charged your watch 29

Check your watch's battery health 29

Stop applications from refreshing in the background 30

Switch your watch on & off 30

Open an application 31

Always On feature 32

Wake your watch's screen 33

Go back to the clock face 34

Wake up to your last activity 35

Keep your watch display on longer 35

Lock or unlock your watch 36

Unlock your Apple Watch 36

Change your password 36

Disable the passcode 38

Lock your watch manually 38

Wipe your watch after 10 unlock attempts 39

Choose a language or region 39

Change wrists or Digital Crown orientation 41

APPLE WATCH SETTINGS 42

Page |

Open & organize applications on your watch.....42
    Show applications in a list or grid view 42
    Launch applications from the Home Screen ..42
    Open an application from the Apps Switcher.44
    Remove apps from the Apps Switcher............44
    Rearrange your applications in grid format ...45
    Remove an application from your watch........47
View the storage used by applications................48
Adjust application settings.................................48
Get more applications on your watch................49
    Download applications from the Application Store on your watch 49
Tell time on your watch.......................................50
Use the Control Center on your watch 51
    Open or close the Control Centre 52
    Check the Controls Centre status....................52
    Rearrange the Controls Centre 53
    Remove the Control Centre buttons 53
Enable Airplane Mode...54
Use your Apple Watch's flashlight......................56
Use theater mode 57
Activate or deactivate WiFi manually 58

Page |

Enable silent mode 59
Ping and find your phone 60
Ping your watch 62
Focus 62
    Enable or disable Focus 63
    Create your Focus 64
    Select a Focus watch face 64
    Create a Focus schedule 65
    Delete or deactivate a Focus schedule 66
Change the brightness & text size on your watch 67
Change the volume of your watch 68
Change your watch's haptic strength 69
Enable or disable the Digital Crown haptics 70
Use Taptic Time 71
View & respond to notifications on your watch .. 72
    Respond to alerts when they arrive 72
    See your unanswered notifications 73
    Turn off all notifications on your device 74
    Show notifications on your lock screen 75
Smart Stack 76
    Open the Smart Stack 76

Page |

Add, remove, & customize widgets 77
Manage your Apple ID settings 78
    Edit your personal info 78
    Manage your Apple ID passcode & security ... 79
    View & manage your subscriptions 80
    View and manage your devices 80
See how much time you spend in daylight 81
    Check your time in daylight 81
    Deactivate time in daylight 81
Handwashing feature 82
    Activate Handwashing 82
Connect your Apple Watch to Wi-Fi 83
Pair Bluetooth speakers or headphones to your watch 84
Handoff tasks from your watch 85
Unlock your phone with your watch 87
Setup and use mobile service 88
    Add your watch to your mobile plan 88
    Transfer your existing mobile plan to your new watch 89
    Activate or deactivate cellular 90
    Check your mobile data usage 91

Page |

Use the calculator app to divide the check and calculate a tip 91
Create an emergency medical ID 92
    Setup your medical information 92
    Check your medical ID on your watch 93
Use your watch to contact emergency services .. 94
    Contact emergency services 94
    End an emergency call 96
    Update your emergency address 96
The Fall Detection feature 97
Crash Detection 99
    Enable or disable Crash Detection 100
Capture a screenshot of your watch 100
SIRI 102
How to use Siri 102
Change Siri's voice feedback settings 103
Type to Siri 104
Erase Siri's history 105
WATCH FACES 106
Enter the Face Gallery 107
Customize a watch face 108
Add complications 108

Add a face 108
Personalize the watch face on your Watch 109
    Select a different watch face 109
    Add complications to your watch face 110
    Add a watch-face to your collection 111
    Check out your collection 111
    Delete a face from your collection 112
    Set the watch ahead 113
Share a watch face 113
Receive a watch face 114
ACTIVITY APPLICATION 115
    Begin 115
    See how you are doing 115
    View your weekly summary 117
    Change your goals 117
    Look at your activity history 118
    View your trends 118
    Check your prizes 119
    See your workout history 120
    Control activity reminders 121
    Suspend daily coaching 121

ALARM 122
  Set an alarm... 122
  Disable the Snooze feature 123
  Delete an alarm 124
  Use your device as a nightstand clock with alarm
  124
BLOOD OXYGEN 126
  Setup blood oxygen 126
  Deactivate background measurement in Theater mode & Sleep mode.. 127
  Measure your blood oxygen level 127
  Check your Blood Oxygen measurement history
  129
CYCLE TRACKING APPLICATION 130
  Setup Cycle Tracking 130
  Log your cycle 131
  Get retrospective ovulation estimates 132
    Configure wrist temperature monitoring 132
    Deactivate wrist temperature 133
CAMERA REMOTE APPLICATION 134
  Snap pictures... 134
  Record videos 135

Page |

Review the photos 135
Select another camera and change the settings 136
COMPASS ON APPLE WATCH 137
Select the type of compass................................. 137
View compass info 140
View your waypoints 141
Add bearings 141
Set a target height warning 142
Use true north 143
If your watch displays a red rotating radar screen 143
Waypoints in the Compass application 144
Configure and show Compass Waypoints 144
Target a waypoint 145
Retrace your steps with Backtrack 145
ECG APPLICATION.. 147
The ECG application 148
Install & setup the ECG application 148
Take an ECG... 150
How to read the results 151
View & share your health info 153
MAPS 155

Page |

Use Walking Radius to see interesting places around you 155

Search the map 156

Find a service close to you 156

View recent locations 157

Pan & zoom 158

Get Directions.. 158

HEART RATE 159

Check your heartrate 159

View your heartrate data graph....................... 159

MINDFULNESS... 161

Begin a Reflect or Breathe Session 161

Set the session duration 162

Change the mindfulness settings 162

Listen to guided Meditations............................ 164

View Meditations you've completed................ 165

MEMOJI 166

Create a Memoji 166

Create a Memoji watch face, edit Memoji, etc.. 167

MUSIC... 169

Add music using your iPhone........................... 169

Add music with your watch 169

Page |

Add a workout playlist.. 170
Remove music using your phone 171
Remove music using your watch...................... 171
Playing songs.. 172
Listen to Apple Music radio 174
STOPWATCH APP 175
Launch & select a stopwatch 175
Begin, end, and reset the stopwatch................ 176
TIMER APP...177
Set a quick Timer..177
Stop or pause a timer 178
Create a custom timer 178
Create multiple timers.................................... 179
NOISE 180
Configure the Noise application 180
Receive noise alerts 181
Disable noise measuring 181
See the details about noise notifications 182
SLEEP APP 183
Setup Sleep on your device............................. 184
Modify or deactivate your next wakeup alarm . 184

Page |

Modify or add sleep schedules 186

Change sleep options... 187

Check your sleep history 188

Check your sleep breathing rate 189

Deactivate breathing rate measurements......... 189

WALKIE-TALKIE 190

Invite your friend to use Walkie-Talkie............ 190

Have a conversation 191

Talk with a tap 192

Remove contacts 192

Make yourself unavailable................................. 193

VOICE MEMOS 194

Record a voice memo 194

Play a voice memo 195

APPLE PAY 196

Add a card to your watch................................... 196

Add cards on your watch 197

Select a default card 197

Rearrange payment cards.................................. 198

Remove a card 198

Find a card's Device Account number............. 199

Edit the transaction information 199
Use your watch to pay for items in a store 200
Make purchases within an application 201
WORLD CLOCK APP 202
Add and remove cities from the World Clock app
.... 202
See the time in other cities 202
Edit cities abbreviations 203
WORKOUT APPLICATION 204
Begin a workout 204
Pause/resume a workout 205
Begin an outdoor push workout 205
Set your status 205
Begin an outdoor push exercise 206
Listen to music while working out 206
Change workout views while working out 207
Customize workouts views 207
Use gym equipment with your watch 208
Check your progress while working out 209
End the workout 210
Review your workout history 210
Begin a swimming workout 210

Page |

Clear water from your watch after swimming 211
See the summary of a swimming exercise 212
Combine many activities in a single workout ... 212
Change your weight & height 213
Automatically pause cycling & running workouts 213
Enable or disable workout reminders 213
Conserve power during workouts 214

RESTART, RESET, RESTORE, AND UPDATE ... 215

Restart your watch 215
    Restart your watch 215
    Force restart your watch 216
Erase your watch 216
    Wipe your Apple Watch and settings 216
Restore your watch from a backup 217
    Backup & restore your watch 217
Update your watch software 218
    Check for and install software updates 218

BOOK INDEX 219

INTRODUCTION

The Apple Watch Series 9 is the latest version of the Apple Watch Series that was first released in 2015. The new device has a faster chip (S9), a brighter screen, a Double-Tap feature, and more. The device is available in 41 mm and 45 mm size options.

FEATURES OF APPLE WATCH SERIES 9

Design

The Apple Watch Series 9 has a rounded & square shape just like the previous generation, and it still comes in 41 mm & 45 mm size options, made to suit your preference and wrist size.

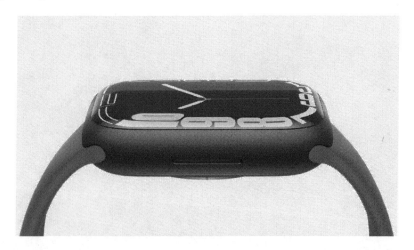

The back of the Apple Watch houses 4 LED clusters & photodiodes which can be used for heart monitoring features like blood oxygen monitoring, EKGs, etc.

The Apple Watch is available in 2 materials: stainless steel, & aluminum.

The weight of each Apple Watch Series 9 model is shown below:

41 mm

- Aluminum: 31.9g
- Stainless steel: 42.3g

45mm

- Aluminum: 38.7g
- Stainless steel: 51.5g

Durability

The Apple Watch Series 9 has an IP6X dust-resistant, which makes it very durable and it can be used in places like deserts or the beach.

The watch still features a WR50 water resistance, rated for immersion in deep water thanks to glue & seals. Due to its 50-meter diving rating, you can swim in a pool or the ocean while wearing your watch. You can use the Apple Watch for shallow-water activities, but it should not be used for scuba diving or other high-speed water-related activities.

Double Tap Gesture

You can use a Double Tap gesture to control your watch. When you tap your index finger and thumb twice, your watch's sensors detect the movement and activate things on the screen, allowing you to perform actions like answer calls, end calls, open notifications, pause or play songs, begin or stop timers, etc.

Battery

The Apple Watch Series 9 has a battery that can last for about 18 hours from one charge (it can last up to 36 hours when Low Power Mode is activated).

Storage space

The Apple Watch Series 9 has 64 GB of storage.

SET UP YOUR APPLE WATCH

Before you begin

- Update your phone to the latest iOS version.
- Ensure your iPhone's Bluetooth is enabled
- Ensure your iPhone is connected to a WiFi or mobile network.

Switch on your watch & wear it

To switch on your device, just long-press the side button till you see the Apple symbol. Then wear your watch.

Bring your watch near your phone

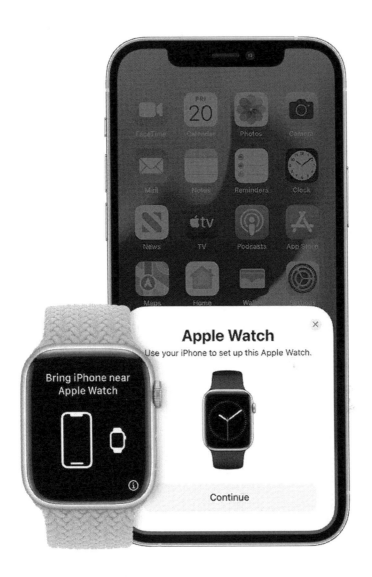

Wait for your iPhone to display the "Use iPhone to setup this watch" notification, then touch the "Continue" button. If your iPhone does not display this message, launch the Watch application on your iPhone, touch the All Watches button, and then touch the Add Watch button.

If this watch belongs to you, click on the Setup for Myself option. Or click on the Setup for Family Member option, and then adhere to the instructions on your display to setup the watch for a member of your family.

Ensure your watch is close to your iPhone during setup

Hold your phone over the animation on your watch

Use your iPhone to scan your watch's face. Wait for your watch to notify you that it has been paired with your phone.

If you cannot use your iPhone's camera, if your watch does not display the pairing animation, or if your phone cannot read it, simply touch the Pair Manually button, and then adhere to the directions on your screen.

Setup as a new device or restore from backup

If this is your first watch, click on the Setup as a New Watch option. If prompted, update your device to the latest watchOS version.

If you have paired another Apple Watch with your current iPhone, a screen will appear that says "Make This Your New Watch ". To view how Express Setup sets up your new device, click on Apps & Data and Settings. Then click on the Continue button. Touch the Customize Settings button if you would like to choose how your watch is configured. Then pick a backup from any of your old Apple Watches to restore. Or click on the Setup as New option if you want to completely personalize your new watch's settings.

Your device may need a software update on your phone before you can pair it. If your phone says that an update is available, click on the Update button and wait for the update to complete.

Pick which hand you would like to wear your device on, and then touch the Continue button.

Read the terms and click the Agree button to continue setup.

Log in with your Apple ID

If prompted, insert your Apple ID passcode. If not, you can login later in the Watch application: Click on General> Apple ID, and then log in.

If Find My is not setup on your phone, you will be told to activate Activation Lock.

Create a password for your watch

Click the Create a Password button or the Add Long Password button on your phone, and go to your watch to insert your new code. Touch the <u>Do not Add Password</u> button to skip this step.

Choose your settings

Choose a text size and activate or deactivate the Bold Text option

Your watch will show you the settings it shares with your phone. If you activate features like Diagnostics, WiFi Call, Locations Service, & Find My on your phone, these settings will automatically be activated on your watch.

After that, you can decide to activate other settings. You can even add your personal info like your birthdate.

Select features & applications

You can setup cellular on cellular models

You will be prompted to setup Apple Pay. Then you will be shown how to setup features like automatic watchOS updates, SOS & Activity.

Wait for your device to synchronize

Your device will show the watch face when the setup is complete. Keep your phone and watch near each other so that they can continue to synchronize info in the background.

APPLE WATCH BAND

How to wear your Watch Band

Put on your watch properly—not too loose, not too tight, and with space for your skin to breathe—keeps you comfortable and allows your watch's sensors to do their job. You can tighten the watch band when working out, and loosen it when you are done.

Recommended fit

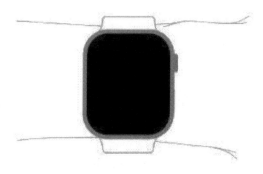

Incorrect fit

Change your watch band

Ensure you're using a band that corresponds to your watch's case size.

- Put your watch face-down in a clean place, such as a microfiber cloth, a soft, etc.
- If you're using a Link Bracelet, press the quick-release button on the bracelet to split the bar into two.

- Press & hold the Release Band button, and then slide the band across to take it off.

- If the watch band does not slide out, press the Release Band button once more and ensure that you hold the button down.

- Ensure the text in the band faces you, then slide the new band in till you feel a click.

Solo Loop or Braided Solo Loop

If you're using a braided Solo Loop or Solo Loop, just drag from the bottom of the band to extend it over your wrist when wearing it or taking it off.

Using the Milanese Loop

To remove the Milanese Loop, simply slide the magnetic closure through the band's connector or the lug.

Conclusion

Don't ever force a band into the slot. If you do not hear or feel a click, try sliding the band to the left, and then to the right. If you've installed the band correctly, it will not move freely until you long-press the band's Release button.

If the band still does not lock, center it, and then slide the band into place. Gently wiggle the band down & up. Do not put on your watch if the band is still sliding.

GET STARTED

Apple Watch Series 9

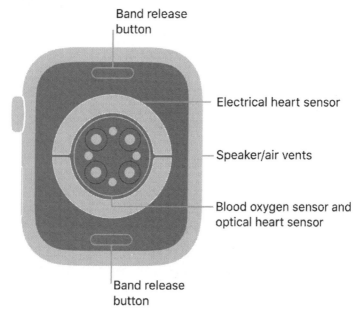

Basic gestures

Here are some gestures that you can use to interact with your watch.

Touch: Gently tap a finger on your watch's display.

Swipe: Move one of your fingers across your watch's display— right, left, down, or up.

Drag: Move one of your fingers across your watch's display without raising the finger.

Use the Double-Tap feature to perform actions on your watch

Tap your thumb and index finger together two times to Answer calls, reply to messages, etc. on your watch. When you use a double-tap, the Double Tap icon will appear in the upper part of your display.

You can select what double-tapping does when browsing your Smart Stack or playing media.

- Navigate to the Settings app, touch Gestures
- Click Double Tap, and then select from the following options:
  ✓ Smart Stack: Choose Select or Advance.
  ✓ Playback: Select Skip or Pause/Play.
- Deactivate Double-Tap if you do not want to use the feature on your watch.

Note: The double-tap feature will not function when Low Power Mode, Sleep Focus, or certain accessibility features are active, or when the screen is inactive because you put your wrist down.

The Apple Watch application

You can use the Watch application on your iPhone to install applications, personalize watch faces, configure the Dock, change settings, etc.

Launch the Apple Watch application

- Click on the Apple Watch app's icon on your iPhone Home Screen.
- Touch the **My Watch** button to view your watch's settings.

Swipe to see your watch face collection.

Settings for Apple Watch.

If you have multiple watches paired to your phone, you'll see the settings for your active watch.

Charge your Watch

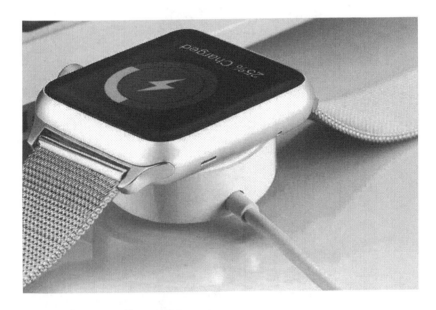

Setup your charger

1. In a place that has good ventilation, place the charging cable or your charger on a flat surface.
2. Connect the charging cable to the power adapter (sold separately)
3. Plug the adapter into a power outlet.

Start charging your Watch

Place the Magnetic Charger on the back of your watch. The concave end of the charging cable will magnetically snap to the back of the watch and align perfectly.

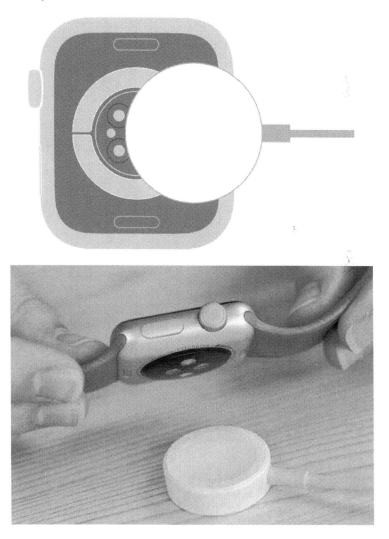

You'll hear a sound when your watch starts to charge (unless the silent mode is active), you'll also see the charge icon⚡ on your watch's face. The icon is red when power is needed, and the icon becomes green when your watch starts charging. The icon turns yellow when Low Power Mode is active.

See the power remaining

To view the power remaining on your watch, press your watch's side button to show the Control Centre.

Save battery power

You can put your watch in Low Power mode to extend the life of its battery. Activating Low Power Mode turns off the Always On feature, background heart-rate & blood oxygen measurement, and heart-rate alerts. Other notifications may be delayed, you may not receive emergency alerts, and some WiFi and mobile connections may be limited. Cellular will be deactivated until you need it—for instance, when steaming songs or sending messages.

Note: The Low Power Mode will turn off when your watch charges to 80 percent.

- Press your watch's side button to show the Control Centre.
- Touch the battery percentage, and then enable **Low Power Mode**.

- Scroll down and click Turn On to confirm your selection.
  You can touch Turn On For, and then select from the available options.

Learn more: If a battery-powered device like an AirPod is connected to your watch via Bluetooth, touch the battery percentage in the Control Centre, and then roll the Digital Crown to view the battery percent of the headphone.

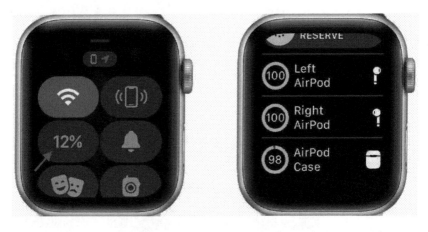

When your watch's battery level drops to 10% or less, your watch will alert you and give you the chance to activate Low Power Mode.

Switch back to normal power mode

- Enter the Control Centre

- Touch the battery percentage, and then disable Low Power Mode.

Check when last you charged your watch

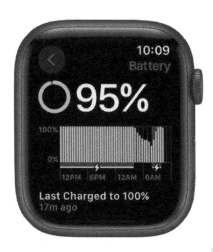

- Launch the Settings application.
- Click on Battery.
  The Battery screen will show the current battery percentage, recent battery charge history, and the last time the battery was charged.

Check your watch's battery health

- Launch the Settings application.
- Click on Battery, and then click on Battery Health.

Stop applications from refreshing in the background

When you switch to another application, the application you were using won't remain open or use systems resources, but it can "refresh" in the background, checking for updates and new contents.

You can disable this option to increase battery life.

- Launch the Settings application.
- Go to General> Background Apps Refresh.
- Disable Background Apps Refresh to stop all applications from refreshing. Or scroll, and then disable refresh for each application.

Switch your watch on & off

Switch on: if your watch is switched off, simply press & hold the side button till the Apple icon shows on the display

The watch face will appear when your watch is turned on.

Switch off: Long-press the side button till you see the sliders on your screen, touch the Power Off icon

⏻ in the upper right, then slide the Power-Off sider to the right end of the screen.

When your watch is switched off, you can long-press the Digital Crown to show the time.

Note: You cannot switch off your watch while it is charging. You have to first remove your watch from its charger before you can switch it off.

Open an application

The Apple Watch comes with many applications. To launch an application, press the Digital Crown to enter the Home Screen and then touch the application's icon. Press the Digital Crown one more time to go back to your watch's Home Screen. You can download more apps from the Apps Store on your watch.

Always On feature

The Always On feature allows your watch to show the watch face & time, even when you put your hands down. When you raise your hand, your watch will function fully.

- Launch the Settings application ⊙.
- Click on Display and Brightness, and then touch Always On.
- Enable the **Always On** setting, then touch any of the options below to set them up:

- ➤ Show Applications.
- ➤ Show Notification.
- ➤ Show Complication Info: Select the complications that display information when you put your wrist down.

Wake your watch's screen

You can wake your watch's screen in the following ways:

- Roll the Digital Crown upward.
- Raise your hand. Your Watch will go back to sleep when you put your wrist down.
- Press the Digital Crown or tap the screen.

If you do not want your watch to wake up when you raise your hand or roll the Digital Crown, launch your watch's Settings application, touch Display and Brightness, and then disable Wake on Crown Rotation or & Wake on Raise Wrist.

Go back to the clock face

You can choose how long your watch stays before returning to the clock face from an open application.

- Enter your watch's Settings application.
- Tap General, touch Return to Clock, and then select one of the available options.

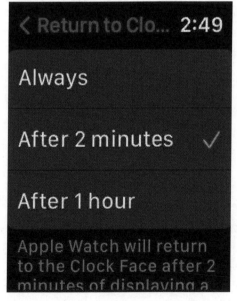

- You can also press the Digital Crown to go back to the clock face.

By default, the settings you choose apply to all applications, but you can choose specific times for each application. To do this, touch one of the applications on this screen, touch the **Custom** button, and then select one of the settings.

Wake up to your last activity

For selected applications, you can configure your watch to go back to the last activity you were doing on it before it went to sleep.

- Launch the Settings application.
- Touch General, touch Return to Clock, scroll down and touch one of the apps, then activate the **Return to App** setting.

Or, launch the Watch application on your phone, then head over to General > Return to Clock.

Keep your watch display on longer

- Launch your watch's Settings application.
- Touch Display and Brightness, click on the **Wake Duration** button, and then touch Wake for 70 Seconds.

Lock or unlock your watch

Unlock your Apple Watch

You can enter the passcode you created to manually unlock your watch, or set it to open automatically when you unlock your smartphone.

- Insert your passcode: Wake your watch, and then insert your password.
- Open your watch when you unlock your smartphone: Enter the Watch application on your phone, touch the **My Watch** button, touch the Passcode button, and activate the **Unlock with iPhone** setting.
  Your phone and watch have to be within the standard Bluetooth range (10m) for the feature to function.

Change your password

Adhere to the instructions below to change the passcode you created when setting up your watch:

- Enter your watch's Settings application.
- Touch the **Passcode** button, touch Change Passcode, and adhere to the directives on the screen.

Or, navigate to the Watch application on your phone, click on the **My Watch** button, touch Passcode, touch Change Passcode, and adhere to the directives on the screen.

Learn more: To use a password that is longer than 4-digits, enter your watch's Settings application, touch the Passcode button, and then disable Simple Passcode.

Disable the passcode

- Enter your watch's Settings application.
- Touch Passcode, and then click on Turn Off Passcode.

Or, navigate to the Watch application on your phone, click on the **My Watch** button, click on Passcode, and then click on Turn Off Passcode.

Lock your watch manually

- Press your watch's side button to enter the Controls Centre.
- Touch the Lock button 🔒.

Note: You must disable the Wrist Detection feature if you want to lock your watch manually. (Launch your watch's Settings application, touch Passcode, and then disable Wrist Detection.)

Wipe your watch after 10 unlock attempts

You can set your watch to erase your info after ten consecutive attempts to unlock it with the wrong password.

- Launch your watch's Settings application.
- Touch the **Passcode** button, and then enable Erase Data.

Choose a language or region

- Launch the Watch application on your iPhone
- Touch the **My Watch** button, head over to General> Language and Region, touch the

Custom button, and then select one of the languages.

To add a language, touch the **Add Language** button, and then choose one of the available options.

Change wrists or Digital Crown orientation

If you want to wear your watch on your other hand or you like the Digital Crown on the other side, change the orientation setting so that you can wake your watch when you raise it, and rolling the Digital Crown moves things the way you want it.

- Launch your watch's Settings application.
- Head over to General> Orientation.

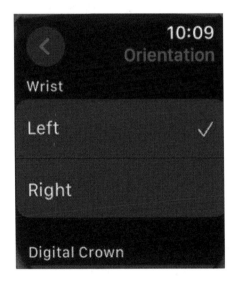

APPLE WATCH SETTINGS

Open & organize applications on your watch

Your watch's Home Screen allows you to launch any application on your device. The Apps Switcher provides fast access to the applications you have used recently.

Show applications in a list or grid view

Your watch's Home Screen can show applications in a list or grid format. To choose one, adhere to the directives below:

- From the watch face, press the Digital Crown to enter the Home Screen.
- Roll the Digital Crown to scroll down, then select List View or Grid View.

Or enter your watch's Settings application, touch App View, and then choose one of the options.

Launch applications from the Home Screen

How you launch an application depends on the view you are using.

- Grid format: Touch the app's icon. Roll the Digital Crown to check out more applications.

From the watch face, press to see the Home Screen.

Tap to open an app.

- List view: Roll the Digital Crown, and then touch one of the applications.

Turn the Digital Crown to browse the apps.

Tap to open an app.

Press Crown Digital once to go back to the Home screen from an application, and then press it one more time to go to the watch face.

Open an application from the Apps Switcher

- Press the Digital Crown twice quickly, and then roll the Digital Crown to scroll through the applications you've used recently.
- Click on an application to launch it.

Turn the Digital Crown to see more apps. Tap one to open it.

Remove apps from the Apps Switcher

Press the Digital Crown twice quickly, then roll the Digital Crown to the application you plan on removing. Swipe the application to the left, then click on **X**.

Swipe left on an app, then tap the X.

Rearrange your applications in grid format

- Click the Digital Crown to enter the Home Screen.
  If the screen is in list view, scroll to the end of the page, and then touch the **Grid View** button. Or enter your watch's Settings applications, touch App View, and then click on the **Grid View** button.
- Long-press an application, and then drag the application to another location on the screen.
- Click the Digital Crown when you are done.

Touch and hold an app, then drag to a new location.

Alternatively, launch the Watch application on your Phone, touch the **My Watch** button, touch Apps View, and then touch Arrangement. Long-press an app's icon, then drag the application to another location on your screen.

Remove an application from your watch

Long-press the Home screen, then touch the **X** on an application to remove the application from your device. The app would remain on your paired iPhone unless you remove the application from your phone too.

In the list format, you can swipe left on an application, then click on the Trash icon to remove it from your watch.

Note: Not every app can be removed from your watch.

View the storage used by applications

See how the storage space on your device is being used.

- Launch the Settings application on your watch.
- Head over to General> Storage.

 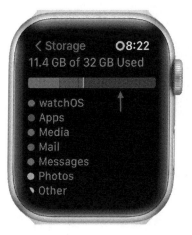

Adjust application settings

- Enter the Watch application on your phone
- Click on the **My Watch** button, and then scroll down to view the applications you've installed.
- Touch an application to adjust its settings.

Get more applications on your watch

The Apple Watch has a variety of applications for communication, health, wellness, and time management. You can also install 3rd-party applications on your phone and get new applications from the Apps Store, either on your watch or from your phone.

Note: To automatically download the iOS version of an application you added on your watch, launch the Settings application, touch Apps Store, and then enable **Automatic Downloads**. To get the latest version of your watch applications, ensure Automatic Updates is also enabled.

Download applications from the Application Store on your watch

- Launch the Apps Store application.
- Roll the Digital Crown to view the applications.
- Click on one of the categories to view more applications.
- Touch Get to get a free application. Click on the price to purchase an application.

If the Re-download button⟲ is displayed instead of a price, it means you have already bought the application and can download it for free. Some applications require that your iPhone also have an iOS version.

To look for a specific application, touch the Search icon🔍 in the upper left part of your display, then type, or use dictation or Scribble to enter the app's name.

Tell time on your watch

There are many ways to tell time on your watch.

- Raise your hand: The time will appear on your watch face, in the clock in grid view, and in the upper right corner of most applications.
- Feel the time: If you want to feel the time tapped on your wrist when your watch is in silent mode, launch the Settings application, touch the **Clock** button, touch Taptic Time, activate Taptic Time, and then select one of the available options.
- Utilize Siri: Raise your hand & say, "What's the time?"
- Hear the time: Launch your watch's Settings application, click on the Clock button, and enable Speak Time. Hold 2 of your fingers on the watch face to hear the time.
  Your watch can play chimes on the hour. Enter the Settings application, touch the **Clock** button, and then activate Chimes. Touch Sounds to select one of the options.

Use the Control Center on your watch

The Controls Centre makes it easier to turn your watch to a flashlight, check your watch's battery, mute your watch, etc.

Open or close the Control Centre

Apple Watch   Apple Watch with Cellular

Touch and hold the bottom, then swipe up to open Control Center.

- Open the Controls Centre: Press your watch's side button.
- Close the Control Centre: Press the side button one more time.

Check the Controls Centre status

Little icons in the upper part of the Controls Centre show the status of certain settings, such as whether Apple Watch is using a cellular connection, an app is using your location, etc.

Open the Control Centre to see the status icons. Touch the icons to get more information.

Rearrange the Controls Centre

Adhere to the instructions below to rearrange the buttons in the Controls Centre:

- Press your watch's side button to reveal the Controls Centre.
- Scroll to the end of the Controls Centre, and then touch the **Edit** button
- Long-press any of the icons/buttons, and then drag it to another location on your screen.
- Touch the **Done** button when you are done.

Remove the Control Centre buttons

Adhere to the instructions below to remove the buttons in the Controls Centre:

- Press your watch's side button to reveal the Controls Centre.
- Scroll to the end of the Controls Centre, and then touch the **Edit** button
- Touch the Remove icon ⊖ in the corner of a button.
- Touch the **Done** button when you are done.

To restore a deleted button, press the side button to reveal the Controls Centre, touch the **Edit** button, and then click on the Add icon ⊕ in the corner of the button. When you're done, simply touch the **Done** button.

Enable Airplane Mode

By default, activating Airplane mode disables cellular & WiFi and keeps Bluetooth activated. But, you can change which settings are activated or deactivated when you enable Airplane Mode.

- Activate Airplane Mode on your device: Press your watch's Side button to enter the Controls Centre, and then touch the Airplane Mode button ✈.

Turn Airplane Mode on or off.

- Put your phone & watch in Airplane Mode in one step: Enter the Watch application, touch the **My Watch** button, head over to General> Airplane mode, and then enable **Mirror iPhone**. When your watch & phone are within Bluetooth range (about 10m), anytime you activate Airplane mode on either device, the other activates it as well.
- Change which settings are enabled or disabled in Airplane Mode: Enter your watch's Settings application, touch Airplane Mode, and then choose whether to activate or deactivate Bluetooth or WiFi by default when you activate Airplane Mode.

To enable or disable Bluetooth or WiFi while your watch is in Airplane Mode, enter the Settings application, then touch Bluetooth or WiFi.

Page | 55

When Airplane Mode is activated, you will see the Airplane Mode symbol in the upper part of your screen.

Note: Even with the **Mirror iPhone** feature activated, you must disable Airplane Mode separately on your watch and phone.

Use your Apple Watch's flashlight

- Turn on the flashlight: Press your watch's side button to enter the Controls Centre, and then touch the Flashlight button . Swipe to pick another mode.

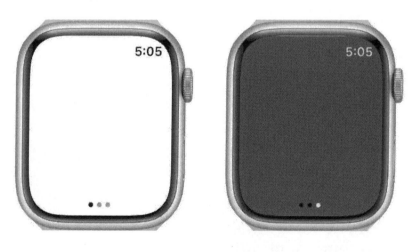

- Adjust brightness: roll the Digital Crown down or up.
- Turn off the flashlight: Press the side button or Digital Crown.

Use theater mode

Theater mode stops your watch's screen from turning on when you raise your hand. It also activates silent mode and makes Walkie-Talkie unavailable.

Press your watch's side button to enter the Controls Centre, click the Theater Mode button , and then touch Theater Mode.

Turn theater mode on or off.

When theater mode is active, the Theater Mode symbol 🎭 will appear in the upper part of your display.

To wake your watch when theater mode is enabled, simply roll the Digital Crown, press the side button, press the Digital Crown, or tap your screen.

Activate or deactivate WiFi manually

Press your watch's side button to enter the Controls Centre, and then touch the WiFi button 📶.

Learn more: To quickly enter the WiFi settings on your watch, long-press the WiFi button in the Controls Centre.

Enable silent mode

Press your watch's side button to enter the Controls Centre, and then touch the Silent button 🔔.

Alternatively, launch the Watch application on your smartphone, click on the **My Watch** button, touch Sound & Haptics, and then enable Silent Mode.

Learn more: When your watch receives a notification, you can quickly mute it by placing your palm on your watch's screen for about 3 seconds. You will feel a tap to confirm that the mute is active. Ensure you activate the **Cover to Mute** setting—enter the Settings application on your watch, touch Sound and Haptic, and then activate Cover to Mute.

Ping and find your phone

The **Precision Finding** feature allows you to use your watch to ping your nearby iPhone 15 and receive directions to it.

- Press your watch's side button to enter the Controls Centre, and then touch the Ping iPhone button.
  Your phone will play a sound and if your watch is in range, the display will show a general heading and the distance to your phone—for instance, 75ft.

- Touch the Ping iPhone button on your watch's screen to play a sound on your phone as you track it.
- Follow the heading displayed on your watch's screen, and make adjustments when needed.
When you get close to your phone, your watch's screen will turn green and your phone will ping twice.

Learn more: Long-press the Ping iPhone button when you are in a dark place to make your iPhone flash.

Ping your watch

You can use your iPhone (iOS 17) to find your watch if it is close by.

- Launch the Settings application on your phone.
- Touch Control Centre, scroll down, and then touch the Add icon ⊕ beside Ping My Watch.
- To ping your watch, simply swipe down from the upper right corner of your iPhone's screen to enter the Controls Centre, and then touch the Ping button ⌖.

Focus

The **Focus** setting helps you stay focused when you want to concentrate on a task. Focus can help you to reduce distractions - it allows you to take just the messages you want to get (the ones that match what you are working on) and let applications & people know you are busy.

You can pick from the available Focus options, for instance, Work, Sleep, Personal, etc. Or, you can create one for yourself on your phone.

Note: To share your Focus settings across all the devices you sign in with the same Apple ID, launch the Settings application on your phone, touch Focus, scroll down, and then enable the **Share Across Devices** feature.

Enable or disable Focus

- Press your watch's side button to reveal the Controls Centre.
- Long-press the current Focus button and then touch one of the Focus options.
If there's no active focus, the Controls Centre will show the DND button .

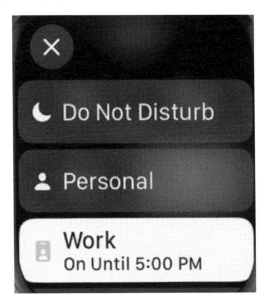

- Select one of the Focus options—On, On for an hour, etc.

To disable a Focus, simply touch its button in the Controls Centre.

When a Focus mode is enabled, the Focus icon will appear in the upper part of your watch face, beside the time in applications, and in the Controls Centre.

Create your Focus

- Enter the Settings application on your phone and touch the **Focus** button.
- Touch the Add icon ✛, select one of the Focus options, and then adhere to the guidelines on your screen.
  You can select a colour and an icon to represent the focus mode you are creating and add a name for it.

Select a Focus watch face

You can set your watch to display a specific watch face when a certain Focus mode is activated. For instance, when the Work Focus mode is enabled, your watch can show the Breathe watch face.

- Enter the Settings application on your phone, and then touch Focus
- Touch one of the Focus options, and then touch Choose under Apple Watch Image.
- Choose one of the watch faces, and then touch the **Done** button.

Create a Focus schedule

You can set your watch to activate a Focus mode at the time of your choice. You can also set a Focus mode to activate at different times of the day. For instance, you can schedule the Work Focus to begin at 9:45 am and end at 12.pm Mondays to Fridays. From 12pm to 1pm you can choose to have no focus. Then start the Work Focus again from 1.pm to 4:30pm Mondays to Thursdays.

- Launch he Settings application on your watch.
- Touch the Focus button, touch one of the Focus modes—Work, for instance— then touch the **Add New** button
- Touch the From & To field and insert when you want the Focus mode to start and stop
- Scroll down, and then select the days
- Click on the Back icon in the upper left edge of your display to save the Focus

- Repeat these steps to add other focus actions.

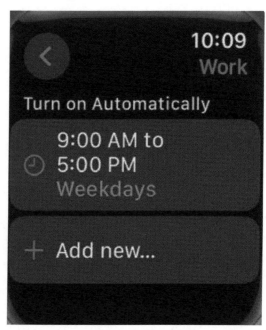

Delete or deactivate a Focus schedule

- Deactivate a Focus schedule: Enter your watch's Settings application, touch the Focus button, and then touch one of the Focus options. Touch one of the schedules, scroll down, and then deactivate **Enabled**.
  Activate **Enabled** when you want to reactivate the schedule
- Delete a Focus schedule: Enter your watch's Settings application, touch Focus, and then touch

one of the Focus options. Touch a schedule, scroll down, and then touch the **Delete** button.

Change the brightness & text size on your watch

Enter your watch's Settings application, and then touch **Display and Brightness** to change the below:

- Brightness: Touch the Brightness control to change the brightness rate, or touch the slider, and then roll the Digital Crown.
- Bold text: Enable Bold Text.

- Text size: Touch Text Size, and then touch the letters or roll the Digital Crown.

Or, launch the Watch application on your phone, touch the **My Watch** button, click on Display and Brightness, and then change the text and brightness.

Change the volume of your watch

- Enter your watch's Settings application.
- Click on the **Sound & Haptics** button.
- Touch the volume control in the Alert Volume segment, or touch the slider, and then roll the Digital Crown.

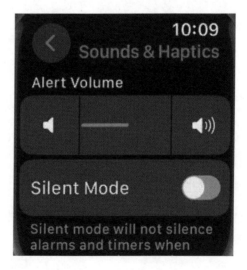

Or, enter the Watch application on your phone, touch Sound & Haptics, and then slide the Alert Volume slider.

Change your watch's haptic strength

You can change the haptics intensity—or wrist taps—your watch uses for alerts.

- Enter your watch's Settings application.
- Click on the **Sounds & Haptic** button and then enable Haptic Alert.
- Select one of the available options.

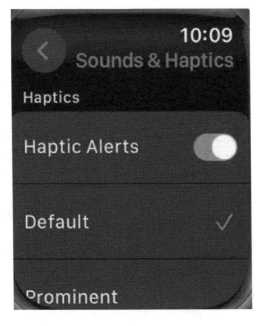

Or, enter the Watch application on your phone, touch the **My Watch** button, touch Sound & Haptic, and then choose one of the options.

Enable or disable the Digital Crown haptics

You feel clicks when you roll the Digital Crown to scroll. Adhere to the following instructions to enable or disable these haptics:

- Enter your watch's Settings application.
- Touch Sounds & Haptic, and then enable or disable Crown Haptics.
  You can also enable or disable system haptics.

Or, launch the Watch application on your phone, touch the **My Watch** button, touch the **Sound & Haptics** button, and then enable or disable Crown Haptics.

Use Taptic Time

When you put your device in silent mode, it can tap out the time on your wrist.

- Launch your watch's Settings application.
- Touch the **Clock** button, scroll down, and then click on the **Taptic Time** button.
- Activate Taptic Time, then select one of the settings—Morse Code, Terse, or Digits.
    - ✓ Digits: Your device will long tap you for every ten hours, short tap you for each hour that follows, long tap you for every ten minutes, and then short tap you for each minute that follows.
    - ✓ Terse: Your device will long tap you for every 5 hours, short tap you for the remaining hours, and then long tap you for every quarter hour.
    - ✓ Morse Code: Your device will tap each digit of the time in Morse code on your wrist.

View & respond to notifications on your watch

The applications on your watch can send you notifications. Your watch can show the notifications when it receives them, but if you do not have time to read them at that moment, you can check back later.

Respond to alerts when they arrive

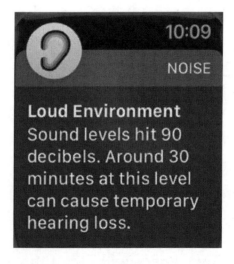

- When your watch receives a notification you'll either feel or hear it. When you do, simply raise your hand to see it.
  The notification can appear in any of the following formats:

✓ A banner in the upper part of your screen
  ✓ A full-screen notification.
- Touch the notification to go through it.
- Swipe down on a notification to clear it. Or scroll to the end of the message, and then touch the **Dismiss** button.

See your unanswered notifications

If you did not check a notification when you received it, it will be stored in the Notification Centre. A red dot in the upper part of your watch indicates that there's an unread message. To view it, adhere to the directives below:

Swipe down to view unread notifications.

- From your watch-face, swipe down to open the Notifications Centre. From any other screen, long-press the upper part of your display, and then swipe down.
Note: You cannot enter the Notifications Centre from your watch's Home Screen. Instead, click the Digital Crown to return to the watch face or launch an application, and then open the Notifications Centre.
- Rotate the Digital Crown to scroll through the notifications list.
- Touch one of the notifications to read or reply to it.

To remove a notification from the Notifications Centre without reading the message, swipe the notification to the left, and then click on the **X** button. To delete all your notifications, scroll to the top of your display and then touch the **Clear All** button.

Learn more: To stop the red dot from showing on your watch face, launch the Settings application, touch the **Notifications** button, and then disable Notification Indicator.

Turn off all notifications on your device

Press your watch's side button to enter the Controls Centre, and then touch the Silent Mode button 🔔.

You'll still feel a tap when your watch receives a notification. Adhere to the directives below to prevent taps and sound:

- Press your watch's side button to enter the Controls Centre, and then touch the DND button 🌙 or the active Focus mode.
- Touch Do Not Disturb, and then pick one of the options—On, On for an hour, etc.

Show notifications on your lock screen

You can choose how notifications appear on your lock screen.

- Enter the Settings application.
- Touch the **Notifications** button
- Select from any of the options below:
  - ➢ Show Summary when Locked: This option allows your watch to show a notification summary when it is locked.
  - ➢ Show Notifications on Wrist Down.
  - ➢ Tap to Show Full Notifications: When you lift your hand to view an alert, you'll see a

summary, followed by the full details after some seconds.

Smart Stack

Smart Stacks are sets of widgets that use info like your location, the time, and your activity to automatically show relevant widgets at the right time of the day. For instance, in the morning, your watch will display the weather forecast or, when you want to travel, your watch will display boarding passes from the Wallet application.

Open the Smart Stack

- Press your watch's Digital Crown to go to the watch face if it's not showing.
- Roll the Digital Crown to scroll down till you reach the Widgets section.
- Scroll to one of the widgets, and then touch it to launch its associated application.

Learn more: At the end of the Smart Stack, you'll find a widget with 3 featured applications— Message, Workouts, & Music. Click on any of the applications to launch it.

Add, remove, & customize widgets

The Smart Stack consists of a set of preconfigured widgets that can be added, removed, and rearranged. Scroll down from the watch face, long-press the Smart Stack, and then carry out any of the below:

- Add widgets: Touch the Add icon ✛, and then touch one of the featured widgets or touch an application that appears under All Apps. Some applications have multiple widgets.
- Remove Widgets: Touch the Remove icon ⊖.

- Pin & unpin a widget: Click on the Pin icon on the widget. To unpin the widget simply tap the Unpin icon on the widget.

Touch the **Done** button when you're done.

Manage your Apple ID settings

You can change the info associated with your Apple ID.

Edit your personal info

- Enter your watch's Settings application.
- Touch [Your Name], click on Personal Information, and then do any of the below:
    ✓ Change your name: Touch your name, then touch the Last, Middle, or First button.
    ✓ Edit your birthday: Touch the **Birthday** button, and then make the needed changes,
    ✓ Receive notifications, offers, or the Apple News newsletter: Touch the **Communication Preference** button. You can activate recommendations for

applications, TV, songs, etc.; or subscribe to the Apple News Newsletter.

Manage your Apple ID passcode & security

- Enter your watch's Settings application.
- Touch [your name], and then touch Sign-In & Security.
  The phone number and e-mail address associated with your Apple ID are shown with their status, for instance, Verified or Primary.
- Carry out any of the below:
  ✓ Remove a verified e-mail address: Touch the address, and then click on the **Remove E-mail Address** button.
  ✓ Add an email address and phone number: Touch the **Add Email or Phone Number** button, select Add email address or phone number, click on the **Next** button, insert your info, and then touch the **Done** button.
  ✓ Change your Apple ID passcode: Touch the **Change Password** button, and then adhere to the guidelines on your display.
  ✓ Change or add a trusted phone number: Click on the **Two-Factor Authentication** button, touch the trusted phone number, verify when asked to, and then touch the **Remove Phone**

Number button. To add more trusted numbers, touch the **Add a Trusted Phone Number** button.
- ✓ Receive verification codes to log in to iCloud.com or another device: Touch the **Two-Factor Authentication** button, and then touch the **Verification Code** button.

View & manage your subscriptions

- Enter your watch's Settings application.
- Touch [your name].
- Click on the **Subscriptions** button and then scroll down to view your subscriptions (active & expired).
- Touch one of the subscriptions to check its cost and length and adjust its options.
- Touch the **Cancel Subscription** button to cancel your subscription.

To re-subscribe to an expired subscription, simply tap it, then choose one of the subscription options.

View and manage your devices

- Enter your Watch's Settings application.
- Touch [your name].

- Scroll down, and then touch one of the devices to show info about it.
- Touch the **Remove from Account** button if you do not recognize the device.

See how much time you spend in daylight

Your watch has a sensor that estimates how much time you spend outside each day.

Check your time in daylight

- Launch the Health application on your phone.
- Touch the **Browse** button, and then touch **Other Data**.
- Touch Time in Daylight.

Deactivate time in daylight

- Enter your watch's Settings application.
- Head over to Privacy & Security> Health
- Touch Time in Daylight, and then deactivate Time in Daylight.

Or, enter the Watch application on your phone, touch the **My Watch** button, touch Privacy, and then disable Time in Daylight.

Handwashing feature

Your device can detect when you start washing your hands and will prompt you to continue washing for twenty seconds.

Activate Handwashing

- Enter your watch's Settings application.
- Click on the Handwashing button, and then enable Handwashing Timer.

If your device notices that you have started washing your hands, it will begin a twenty-second timer.

Connect your Apple Watch to Wi-Fi

Connecting your device to a WiFi network allows you to use many of its features, even when your phone is not with you.

Select a WiFi network

- Press your watch's side button to open the Controls Centre.
- Press & hold the WiFi button 🛜, and then touch the WiFi network's name.
- If the network requires a passcode, use your watch's keyboard to enter the passcode. Or, click on the Password icon 🔑 and select one of the passwords from the list. You can also use your iPhone's keyboard to insert the passcode.
- Click on the Join button.

Forget a network

- Press your watch's side button to reveal the Controls Centre.
- Long-Press the Wi-Fi button 🛜, and then touch the name of the network you connected to.
- Touch the **Forget This Network** button.

Pair Bluetooth speakers or headphones to your watch

You'll need a headset or Bluetooth speakers to listen to most of the sounds on your device. Adhere to the directions that came with the speakers or headset to place it in discovery mode. When the Bluetooth device is ready, follow the steps below:

- Enter your watch's Settings application, and then touch the **Bluetooth** button.
- Touch the device when it pops up on your screen.

Monitor & change your headphone's volume level

- Press your watch's side button to reveal the Controls Centre.
- When listening to a song, podcast, etc., on your headphones, touch the Headphone Volume icon.

  A meter will show the headphone's volume on your screen.
- Click the volume control in the Headphones Volume section, or touch the slider, and then roll the Digital Crown to change the volume level.

Handoff tasks from your watch

The Handoff setting allows you to move from one Apple device to another without losing what you are doing. For instance, while replying to an e-mail through the Mail application on your watch, you can decide to finish answering the email in the Mail application on your phone. To use the Handoff setting, just adhere to the instructions below:

- Unlock your iPhone.
- On a Face ID model, swipe up from the lower edge & stop to reveal the Apps Switcher. (On a Home button model, press the home button two times quickly to open the Apps Switcher.)

- Touch the button in the lower part of the Apps Switcher to continue working in the application.

Learn more: If you can't find the button in the Apps Switcher, ensure Handoff is enabled in your iPhone's Settings app> General> AirPlay & Handoff.

Handoff is enabled by default. To turn it off, enter the Watch application on your phone, touch the **My Watch** button, click on the **General** button, and then deactivate the **Enable Handoff** option.

Unlock your phone with your watch

Adhere to the following instructions to use your watch to unlock your iPhone (Face ID model) when something is preventing Face ID from recognizing you:

- Enter the Settings app on your phone, touch the **Face ID & Passcode** button, and insert your password.
- Scroll to the Unlock with Apple Watch section, and then activate the setting for your device.
  If you have many watches, activate the setting for each of them.
- To unlock your phone, ensure you are putting on your watch, wake your phone, and look at the display.
  Your watch will tap your wrist to inform you that your phone has been unlocked.

Note: To open your locked phone, your watch needs to have a password, be unlocked & on your wrist, and be near your phone.

Setup and use mobile service

With a cellular model Apple Watch and a mobile connection to the carrier your iPhone uses, you can make calls, answer messages, stream songs, etc., even when you are not connected to WiFi or you do not have your iPhone with you.

Add your watch to your mobile plan

Adhere to the directives on your screen during initial setup to activate mobile service on your watch. To activate the feature later, simply adhere to the directives below:

- Enter the Watch application on your phone.
- Touch the **My Watch** button, and then touch the **Cellular** button.

Adhere to the directives on your display to get more info about your mobile service plan and activate cellular for your watch.

Transfer your existing mobile plan to your new watch

Adhere to the directives below to transfer your mobile plan from one Apple Watch (cellular model) to another Apple Watch (cellular model):

- While putting on your watch, launch the Watch application on your phone.
- Touch the **My Watch** button, touch the **Cellular** button, and then touch the Info icon ⓘ beside the cellular plan.
- Click on Remove [carrier's name] Plan, and then confirm the choice you've made.

You can contact your carrier to remove this watch from your mobile plan.
- Remove your old Apple Watch from your wrist, wear the other one, touch the **My Watch** button on your phone, and then touch the **Cellular** button.

Adhere to the directions on your display to activate your device for cellular.

Activate or deactivate cellular

- Press your watch's side button to enter the Controls Centre.

- Click on the Cellular button , and then activate or disable Cellular.

The green bars at the upper part of the Controls Centre indicate the mobile connection status.

Check your mobile data usage

- Enter your watch's Settings application.
- Click the Cellular button, then scroll down to see how much data you have used so far.

Use the calculator app to divide the check and calculate a tip

- Launch the Calculator application
- Insert the total bill amount, and click on the **Tip** button.
- Roll the Digital Crown to select the tip's percentage.
- Click on People, then roll the Digital Crown to enter the number of individuals that want to share the bill.
  You would see the tip amount, total amount, and how much everyone owes

Create an emergency medical ID

A medical ID provides info that may be helpful in an emergency, such as medical conditions, and more. Your device can provide this information to anyone attending to you in an emergency.

Setup your medical information

- Enter the Health application on your phone.

- Click on your profile photo in the upper right corner of your display, and then touch the **Medical ID** button.
- Touch the Edit button or the Get Started button, and then fill in your details.
- Touch Add Emergency Contacts in the Emergency Contacts segment, and then add the contacts.
- Click on the **Done** button.

Check your medical ID on your watch

- Press your watch's side button till the sliders show up.
- Slide the Medical ID slider to the right end.

 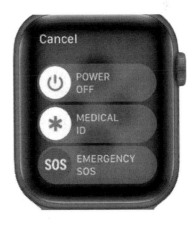

- Touch the **Done** button when you are done.

Or, enter your watch's Settings application, then head over to SOS> Medical ID.

Use your watch to contact emergency services

In an emergency, you can use your device to call for help.

Contact emergency services

Do one of the below:

- Press your watch's side button till the sliders show up, and then slide the Emergency Call slider to the right end.

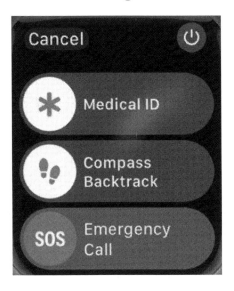

Your device will call the emergency services in your area, such as 911 (In some areas, you may have to press a number on the keypad to make the call.)
- Long-press the side button till your device plays a warning sound and begins a countdown. Your watch will call emergency services after the countdown ends. Your device will play this warning sound even when you put it in silent mode, so if you are in an emergency and do not

want to make a sound, use the emergency call slider.

If you do not want your device to automatically begin an emergency countdown when you long-press the Side button, disable the **Auto-Dialing** feature. Enter your watch's Settings application, touch SOS, touch Hold Side Button, and then disable Hold Side Button.

- Say "Siri" or "Hey Siri, call [emergency service's number, for example 911]."
- Enter the Message application on your device, touch the **New Message** button, click on the **Add Contact** button, touch the number pad button, and then type 911. Touch the **Create Message** button, write what you want, and then touch the Send button.

End an emergency call

If you mistakenly start an emergency call, touch the End button , and then touch the **End Call** button to cancel the call.

Update your emergency address

If the emergency services cannot find you, they'll go to your emergency address.

- Launch the Settings application on your phone.
- Head over to Phone> WiFi Calling, touch Update Emergency Address, and then fill in your emergency address.

The Fall Detection feature

If your device detects a hard fall when Fall Detection is turned on, it can help you contact emergency services & send a message to your emergency contact. If your watch detects a hard fall and notices that you've not moved for about 60 seconds after falling. It would tap you, play an alarm, and try to contact emergency services.

If the date of birth you entered when setting up your device shows that you are 55 or older, the Fall Detection feature is automatically enabled. If you are between the ages of 18 & 55, you can enable Fall Detection manually by adhering to the directions below:

- Launch your watch's Settings application.
- Touch SOS, touch Fall Detection, and then activate Fall Detection.

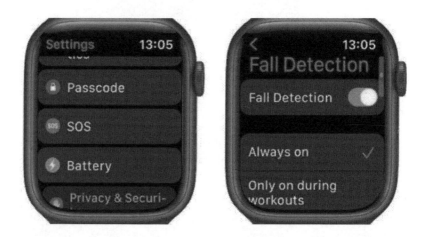

Or, launch the Watch application on your phone, click on the **My Watch** button, click on the **Emergency SOS** button, and then activate Fall Detection.

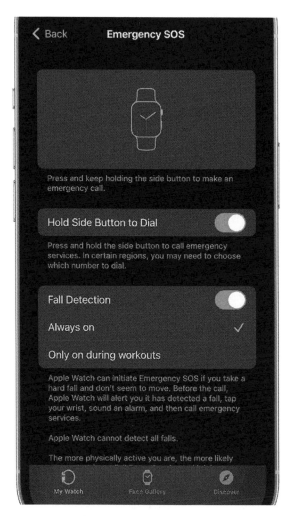

- Select Always On to have Fall detection active always or "Only on during workout" to have it active when you are working out.

Crash Detection

If your device detects a car accident, it can help you contact emergency services and notify your emergency contacts.

When your device detects a car accident, an alert will appear on your screen and it will automatically initiate an emergency phone call after twenty seconds unless you choose to cancel. If you're unresponsive, your device will play a voice message for the emergency services, telling them that you have been involved in a serious car accident and giving them your location details.

Enable or disable Crash Detection

Crash Detection is enabled by default. Adhere to the directions below to disable it:

- Launch your watch's Settings application.
- Touch SOS> Crash Detection, and then deactivate Call After Severe Crash.

Capture a screenshot of your watch

- Enter your watch's Settings application, touch General> Screenshot, and then activate the <u>Enable Screenshots</u> feature.

- Press the side button and Digital Crown simultaneously to capture a picture of your display.

The Screenshots are stored in the Photos application on your phone.

SIRI

Use the Siri feature to perform tasks on your device. For instance, you can use Siri to translate a language you don't understand, identify a song, etc.

In a nutshell, you can use Siri to perform actions that usually take multiple steps.

How to use Siri

Do any of the below to make a Siri request:

- Raise your hand & talk into your watch.

To disable the Raise To Speak feature, launch your watch's Settings application, touch the **Siri** button, and then disable Raise To Speak.

- Say "Siri" or "Hey Siri" then make a request.
  To disable the "Ask Siri" feature, enter your watch's Settings application, click on the Siri button, touch Listen for "Hey Siri" or "Siri" and then select Off.
- Long-press the Digital Crown till the listening indicator appears, then make your request.
  To disable this feature, enter your watch's Settings application, click on the **Siri** button, and then disable **Press the Digital Crown**.

Learn more: After activating Siri and making a request, you can put your hand down. You will feel a tap when a response is available.

To answer a question from Siri or continue the conversation, just long-press the Digital Crown and talk

Note: To make use of Siri, your watch needs to have an internet connection.

Change Siri's voice feedback settings

Siri can speak responses on your device. Launch your watch's Settings application, touch the **Siri** button, click on Siri Response, and then select from the below:

- Always on: Siri would speak out, even when your device is in silent mode.
- Control with Silent Mode: Siri's response is silent when your device is set to silent mode.
- Headphones Only: Siri will only speak out when your device is connected to a Bluetooth headphone.

To change the language & voice used for Siri, enter your watch's Settings application, touch the **Siri** button, and then click on Language or Siri Voice. When you click Siri Voice you can pick from the available voices.

Type to Siri

The **Type to Siri** feature allows you to type your request instead of saying it.

- Enter your watch's Settings application.

- Head over to Accessibility> Siri, and then activate the **Type to Siri** feature.

Erase Siri's history

When you use the **Siri** feature, your requests are saved on Apple's server for 6 months to make Siri's response to you better. You can erase these interactions from the server anytime you want.

- Launch your watch's Settings application.
- Click on the **Siri** button, touch Siri History, and then click on **Delete Siri History**.

WATCH FACES

You can view all the available watch faces in the Face Gallery in the Watch application on your iPhone. If you find one that you like, you can personalize it, select complications, and add the face to your collection.

Tap a face to customize it and add it to your collection.

Enter the Face Gallery

Launch the Watch application on your phone and then click on Face Gallery in the lower part of your display.

Customize a watch face

In the Face Gallery, touch one of the faces, and then click on a feature, like style or colour.

As you try different options, the face at the top will change to ensure that the design is perfect.

Add complications

- In the Face Gallery, click on one of the faces, and then touch the complication position, like Bottom, etc.
- Swipe to view the available complications for a position, and then touch the one you like.
- If you decide you do not need a complication in a position, scroll to the beginning of the list, and then click Off.

Add a face

- In the Face Gallery, click on one of the faces, and then select the complications and features you'd like to add.
- Touch the **Add** button.

The watch face will be added to your collection and it will become your watch's current face.

Personalize the watch face on your Watch

You can personalize watch faces on your Apple Watch.

Select a different watch face

Long-press the current watch face, swipe to any of the available watch faces, and then touch it.

Add complications to your watch face

You can add features known as complications to some watch faces.

- With the current watch face showing, long-press your screen, then touch the **Edit** button.
- Swipe left till you get to the end.
  If a watch face provides complications, you will find them in the last screen.
- Touch any of the complications to choose it and roll the Digital Crown to select a new one - For instance, Heartrate or Activity.
- When you are done, click the Digital Crown to save the adjustments you've made and then touch the face to use it.

Add a watch-face to your collection

Create your collection of personalized faces.

- With the current watch face showing, long-press your screen.
- Swipe left till you get to the Add New Watch Face screen, and then click on the New (+) button.

Tap new, scroll to browse watch faces, then tap a face to add it.

- Roll the Digital Crown to see the watch faces, and then click on the **Add** button.

After adding it, you can personalize the watch face.

Check out your collection

- Enter the Watch application on your phone.
- Touch the **My Watch** button and then swipe through your collection in the My Face segment.

Delete a face from your collection

- With the current watch face showing, long-press your screen.
- Swipe to the face you'd like to delete, then swipe the watch face up, and then touch the **Remove** button.

Swipe up to delete a watch face, then tap Remove.

You can also enter the Watch application on your Phone, touch the **My Watch** button, and then click on Edit in the My Faces area. Click the Remove icon ● beside the watch face you plan on deleting, and then click on the Remove button.

Set the watch ahead

- Launch your watch's Settings application.
- Touch the Clock button
- Touch +0 min, then roll the Digital Crown to set the watch ahead.

This setting will only change the time displayed on the watch face, it does not have any effect on alarms, notification time, or any other time.

Share a watch face

- Go to the watch face you want to share on your watch.
- Long-press your display, and then touch the Share icon.
- Touch the watch face's name, and then touch the "Don't Include" button for any complications you do not want to share.
- Click on a recipient, or click Mail or Message.
  If you touch the Mail or Messages option, add one of your contacts, a subject (for Mail only), and the message.
- Touch the Send button.

Or, launch the Watch application, touch one of the watch faces from your Face Gallery or collection, click on the Share icon, then choose any of the sharing options.

Receive a watch face

- Open a text, e-mail, or a link that has the watch face that was sent to you.
- Touch the Shared watch face, and then touch the Add button.

ACTIVITY APPLICATION

The Activity application monitors your day-to-day activities and motivates you to achieve your fitness goals. The application monitors how many times you stand, how long you workout, & how much you move. 3 rings in different colours sum up your progress. The goal is to complete each ring every day by sitting less, moving more, and exercising.

Begin

When setting up your device, you are asked if you want to setup the Activity application. If you choose not to, you can set it up later when you launch the Activity application.

- Launch the Activity application
- Swipe left to view the Stand, Exercise, & Move description, and then click on the Get Started button.

See how you are doing

Launch the Activity application to see your progress. The Activity application will show 3 rings.

- The blue one displays the number of times you have stood in a day and moved for a minimum of 1 minute in an hour.
- The green one displays how many minutes of exercise you have done.
- The red one displays how many active calories you have burned from moving.

If you've indicated that you're using a wheelchair, the blue Stand ring changes to a Roll ring and shows how many times you have rolled for about 1 minute per hour.

Roll the Digital Crown to view your current total—scroll to view your progress, your total distance, steps, etc.

An overlapping ring means you've passed the target you set for yourself. Touch the Weekly Summary icon to see your progress for the week.

View your weekly summary

- Launch the Activity application
- Touch the Weekly Summary icon

Change your goals

You can change your activity goals if you find them not challenging enough or too difficult.

- Launch the Activity application.
- Touch the Weekly Summary icon
- Scroll to the end of the screen, and then click on the Change Goals button.
- To change a goal, touch the Minus icon or the Add icon, and then click on the "Next" button.
- Touch the Ok button when you are done.

Learn more: To adjust a specific goal, roll the Digital Crown to the goal, and then touch the Change Goal icon

Look at your activity history

- Launch the Fitness application on your phone, and then touch the Summary button.
- Touch the Activity field, touch the Calendar button 🗓, and then touch one of the dates.

View your trends

The Trend Chart displays daily trend data for cardio fitness, walking distance, standing minutes, standing hours, exercise minutes & active calories. Trends compare your ninety days of activity to the past 365 days.

- Launch the Fitness application on your phone
- Touch the Show More button in the Trends section.
- To view the history of a particular trend, simply click on it.

If the Trend arrow displayed for a specific metric points up, it means that you are maintaining or improving your fitness level. A downward-pointing arrow means that the 90-day average for that metric has started declining.

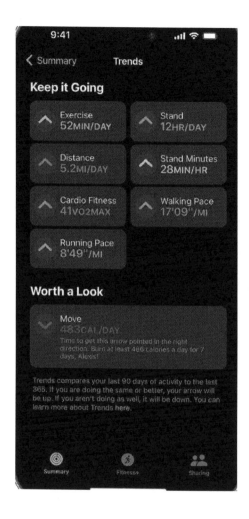

Check your prizes

You can win prizes for personal records, major milestones & streaks using your watch.

- Launch the Activity application

- Touch the Award icon .
- Touch one of the award categories, and then touch any of the awards to get more information about it.

Or, launch the Fitness application on your phone, and then scroll down to the Awards section.

See your workout history

- Launch the Activity application.
- Scroll down to the end of the screen
- Touch a workout to review it.

Control activity reminders

Your watch will inform you when you are on track or lagging behind your goals. Adhere to the directions below to select which reminders and alerts you want to see:

- Launch your watch's Settings application.
- Click on Activity and then setup the notification.

Or, launch the Watch application on your phone, touch the My Watch button, and then touch Activity.

Suspend daily coaching

Adhere to the directions below to disable activity reminders:

- Launch your watch's Settings application.
- Touch Activity, and then disable Daily Coaching.

Or, launch the Watch application on your phone, touch the My Watch button, click on Activity, and then disable Daily Coaching.

ALARM

Use the Alarm application to vibrate or play sound on your device at scheduled times.

Set an alarm

- Launch the Alarms application
- Click the Add Alarm icon ⊕.

- Touch PM or AM, and then touch the minutes or hours.
  The last step isn't necessary when making use of a 24-hour time.

- Roll the Digital Crown to make adjustments, and then touch the Check button ⊘.
- To activate or deactivate the alarm, just touch its switch. Or touch the alarm time to set snooze, repeat, & label options.

Disable the Snooze feature

When the alarm starts playing, you can click on the Snooze button to wait a few minutes before the alarm plays again. If you do not want to allow snooze, adhere to the following directions:

- Launch the Alarms application.
- Touch the alarm in the alarms list, and then disable Snooze.

Delete an alarm

- Launch the Alarms application.
- Touch the alarm from the list.
- Scroll down, and then click on the **Delete** button.

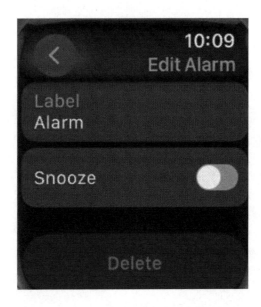

Use your device as a nightstand clock with alarm

- Launch your watch's Settings application.
- Touch General> Nightstand Mode, and then enable Nightstand mode.

When you connect your device to the charger when nightstand mode is activated, it will display the charge status, date & time, and the time of any alarm you have set. To see the time, simply touch your screen or nudge the table.

When the alarm you set starts playing, simply press the side button to disable it or click the Digital Crown to snooze for some minutes.

BLOOD OXYGEN

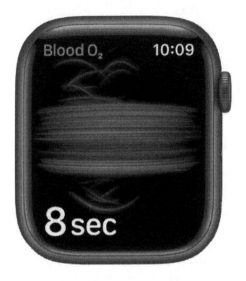

With the Blood Oxygen application, you can measure the percentage of oxygen your red blood cells carry from your lungs to the other parts of your body. Knowing your blood's oxygen levels can help you understand your health and overall well-being.

Setup blood oxygen

- Launch your watch's Settings application.
- Click on the Blood Oxygen button, and then enable Blood Oxygen Measurement.

Deactivate background measurement in Theater mode & Sleep mode

Blood oxygen measurement uses a bright red light that would shine on your wrist, which is more visible in the dark. You can disable measurements if the light is distracting you.

- Enter your watch's Settings application.
- Touch the Blood Oxygen button, and then disable In Theater Mode & In Sleep Focus.

Measure your blood oxygen level

If background measurements are enabled, the Blood Oxygen application will periodically measure your blood oxygen level all through the day, but you can measure it anytime you like.

- Enter the Blood Oxygen application.
- Place your hand on a table or on your lap, and ensure your wrist is flat, with your watch's screen facing up.

- Click on the Start button, and hold your hand firmly for about fifteen seconds.
- You'll get the results after the measurement. Click the Done button.

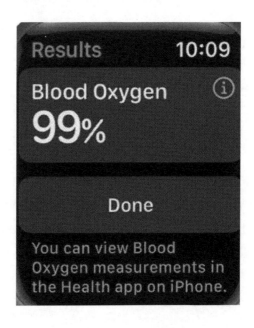

Note: To get the best results, your device needs to touch your skin. Ensure you wear your watch not too loose or tight.

Check your Blood Oxygen measurement history

- Head over to the Health application on your phone.
- Click on the Browse button, click on Respiratory, and then touch Blood Oxygen.

CYCLE TRACKING APPLICATION

You can record details about your menstrual cycle in the Cycle Tracking application. You can enter flow info & record symptoms like cramps, headaches, etc. By using your info, the Cycle Tracking application can alert you when your next fertile window or period is likely to begin. If you wear your device to bed every night, the Cycle Tracking application can use your wrist temperature to make better period predictions and provide ovulation predictions.

Setup Cycle Tracking

- Enter the Health application on your smartphone.
- Click on the **Browse** button to show the Health Category screen.
- Touch Cycle Tracking.
- Touch the Get Started button, and adhere to the guidelines on your display to set notifications & other options.

To remove or add options after configuring Cycle Tracking, launch the Health application, click on the

Browse button, touch the Cycle Tracking button, and then touch Options beside Cycle Log.

Log your cycle

- Launch the Cycle Tracking application.
- Do one of the below:
  - ✓ Record a period on a specific day: With the date displayed on the timeline, click the Log button. Touch Period, click on the flow rate, and then click on the **Done** button.
  - ✓ Record symptoms, or other info: With the date shown in the timeline, click the Log button. Click on one of the categories, select one of the options, and then click on the **Done** button.

Your observations will be displayed in the Cycle log on your phone. If you have activated Fertility & Period Notifications in the Health application on your phone, your watch will notify you about upcoming periods, retrospective ovulation predictions, and fertile window predictions.

You can also record factors that may affect your cycle (like pregnancy, breastfeeding, and birth control) in the Health application on your phone.

Get retrospective ovulation estimates

If you wear your device to bed every night, the Cycle Tracking application can use your wrist temperature to make better period predictions and provide ovulation predictions.

Configure wrist temperature monitoring

- Setup Cycle Tracking and Sleep (in the Sleep application).
- To determine your temperature, make sure you have Sleep Focus on and wear your watch while you sleep.

Your device will provide your wrist temperature data after 5 nights.
- To view wrist temperature info, launch the Health application on your phone, click on the Browse button, touch Body Measurements, and then click on Wrist Temperature.

Your device should be able to provide ovulation predictions after about 2 menstrual cycles of wearing it to bed every night.

Deactivate wrist temperature

- Launch the Health application on your phone, touch the Browse button, and then click on the Cycle Tracking button.
- Scroll down, click on Options, and then disable the Use Wrist Temperature feature.

CAMERA REMOTE APPLICATION

You can set up your iPhone for a video or picture, and then use your watch to snap the picture or record the video remotely. There is a 3-second delay before the shot is captured, giving you enough time to put your wrist down and get ready.

Note: Your watch and phone have to be within Bluetooth range for the Camera Remote to function properly (about 33ft or 10m).

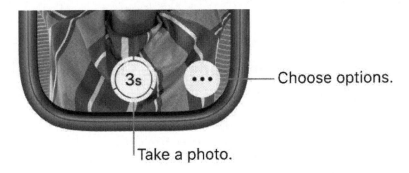

Snap pictures

- Launch the Camera Remote application on your watch.
- Set your phone to take the picture using your watch as the view finder.

Roll the Digital Crown to zoom. To change the exposure level, touch the main area of the picture in the preview image.
- Touch the Shutter button to snap the picture.

The picture will be stored in the Photos application on your phone but you can review it on your watch.

Record videos

- Launch the Camera Remote application on your watch.
- Set your phone to record the video using your watch as the view finder.
Roll the Digital Crown to zoom.
- Press & hold the Shutter to start the recording session.
- Release the Shutter when you want to stop recording.

Review the photos

Do any of the below to review your shots on your watch:

- Check a picture: Touch the thumbnail in the lower-left corner of your display.
- Swipe right or left to view other pictures
- Roll the Digital Crown to zoom in or out.
- Drag on a zoomed picture to Pan
- Double-tap the picture to make it fill the screen.
- Touch your screen to hide or display the Close icon and the number of shots.

Touch the **Close** button when you are done.

Select another camera and change the settings

- Launch the Camera Remote application.
- Click the More Options icon ***, and then pick from the following options:
    - ✓ Timer
    - ✓ Flash
    - ✓ Camera(Back or front)
    - ✓ Live Photo.

COMPASS ON APPLE WATCH

The Compass application displays the direction your watch is facing, as well as your elevation & location. You can create Waypoints in the application and find the direction and distance between them.

Note: If you remove the Compass application from your phone, it will also be deleted from your watch.

Select the type of compass

The Compass application has 5 different versions.

- When you launch the Compass application for the first time, your watch will display your bearing in the middle of the watch face, with waypoints in the inner ring.

- Roll the Digital Crown down to show a big compass arrow with where you are heading under it.

- Roll the Digital Crown up 2 screens to view your coordinates, elevation, and altitude in the compass inner ring. Waypoints that are nearby are displayed in the middle of the compass. While your bearing is displayed in the outer ring.

- Keep rolling the Digital Crown to reveal the locations of the waypoints you've created and also display automatically generated waypoints that show where you've parked, and find out the last place your phone and watch were able to establish a mobile connection.

- Every screen that displays the compass dial has an Elevation icon in the lower part of the screen.

    Click the Elevation icon to display a 3D view of the waypoint elevation based on your current elevation.

View compass info

Launch the Compass application, and then click on the Info icon 🛈 in the upper left corner of your display to show your coordinates, elevation, etc.

View your waypoints

- Launch the Compass application
- Click the Info icon 🛈 in the upper left corner of your display, and then click on the **Waypoints** button.
- Click on the Compass Waypoints button to display the available waypoints.

Add bearings

- Launch the Compass application
- Click the Info icon 🛈 in the upper left corner of your display, and then click on the **Bearing** button.
- Roll the Digital Crown to a bearing, and then click the Check icon ✓.

  To adjust the bearing, touch the Info button 🛈, scroll down, touch the Bearing button, roll the Digital Crown to another bearing, and then touch the Check icon ✓.

- To clear the bearing, touch the Info button 🛈, scroll, and then touch the Clear Bearings button.

Set a target height warning

Set a target height and get an alert when you pass it.

- Launch the Compass application.
- Click the Info button ⓘ, and then click on the Set Target Alert button.
- Roll the Digital Crown to select the target height.

  To adjust the target, touch the Info button ⓘ, touch the Target Alert button, and then select another elevation. To delete the target, touch the Info button ⓘ, and then click on the Clear Target button

Alerts appear when your target level is exceeded.

Use true north

Follow the guidelines below to use true north instead of magnetic north:

- Enter your watch's Settings application
- Click on the Compass button, and then activate Use True North.

If your watch displays a red rotating radar screen

If your watch displays a red rotating radar screen when you launch the Compass application, it could be due to any of the below:

- Your device could be in a poor magnetic environment.
- Location service is deactivated: To enable or disable Location Services, enter your watch's Settings application, click on the Privacy button, and then touch Location Service.
- Compass Calibrations is deactivated: To enable or deactivate Compass Calibration, enter your iPhone's Settings application, touch Privacy and

Security> Location Service, and then touch Systems Settings.

Waypoints in the Compass application

Configure and show Compass Waypoints

You can add your location as a waypoint in the Compass application. You can then view the direction, distance, and elevation of every waypoint you've created.

- Launch the Compass application
- Click on the Waypoint button to add waypoints.
- Fill in the waypoint's info like symbols (For instance house or vehicle), colour, or label, and then touch the Done icon.
- To check your waypoints, touch a waypoint in any of the compass screens, roll the Digital Crown to choose a waypoint, and then touch the Select button
You will see the waypoint's elevation, direction, & distance on your display.

- Click the Edit icon ✏ to change the info about the waypoint you've selected and display the waypoint with its coordinates on a map.

Target a waypoint

Target a compass waypoint to see its elevation, direction, & distance.

- Launch the Compass application
- Click the Info icon ⓘ, click on the Waypoints button, click on the Compass Waypoints button, and then touch one of the waypoints
- Scroll, and then touch the Target Waypoint button

You will see the waypoint's elevation, direction, & distance on your display.

Retrace your steps with Backtrack

You can use the Backtrack feature to track your path, and then retrace your steps if you get lost.

Note: The Backtrack feature is created for use in remote locations, away from the usual places like your house or work, and away from very populated locations.

- Launch the Compass application.
- Click on the Backtrack button 🔘, and then click the <u>Start</u> button to start recording your path.
- To retrace your steps, click on the "Pause" button 🔘, and click on the "<u>Retrace Step</u>" button.
You will see the location where you 1st touched the Backtrack button 🔘 on the compass.
- Follow the route back to go to where you first touched the Backtrack button
- When you are done, touch the Backtrack button 🔘, and then touch the <u>Delete Step</u> button.

ECG APPLICATION

An electrocardiogram test (also known as EKG or ECG) records the intensity & timing of electrical signals that cause a heartbeat. By checking an ECG, a doctor would be able to learn about heart rate and detect abnormalities.

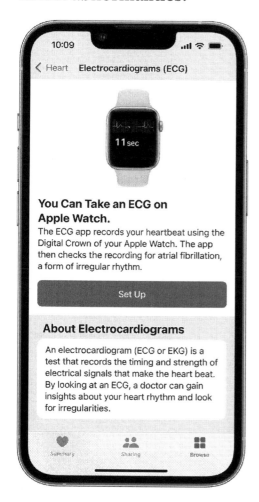

The ECG application

The ECG application can record your heart rate and rhythm with the electric heart sensor on your watch and then check your heart rate record for AFib, a type of abnormal rhythm.

The ECG application shouldn't be used by individuals below 22 years of age.

Install & setup the ECG application

The ECG application is installed when you setup the EKG application in the Health application. Adhere to the directions below to setup the ECG application:

- Launch the Health application on your phone.
- Adhere to the guidelines on your display. If your iPhone doesn't display a prompt to setup ECG, simply touch the "Browse" button, then click on Heart> Electrocardiogram(ECG)> Setup ECG Application.
- After setting up the application, launch the ECG application on your watch to get an ECG test.

If you still cannot find the application on your watch, launch the Watch application on your phone and then click on the Heart button. In the ECG segment, click Install to install the application.

Take an ECG

You can have an ECG whenever you want.

- Ensure you are wearing your watch in the right way.
- Launch the ECG application
- Put your hands on the table or your lap.

- Hold your finger on the Digital Crown. You do not have to press the Digital Crown while checking your EKG.
- Wait for about 30 seconds for the test to be completed. You will be sent a classification after the record, and then you can touch the <u>Add Symptoms</u> button to select your symptoms

- Click on the Save button to highlight any symptoms, and then click on Done.

How to read the results

When you are done with a test, you'll get one of the following results. Regardless of the result you receive, talk to your doctor if you are sick or have symptoms.

Atrial fibrillation

An AFib result implies that the heart beats abnormally. If you are sent an AFib classification and you've not been diagnosed with AFib, talk to your doctor.

Sinus rhythm

If you receive a sinus rhythm result, it implies that your heart beats in a uniform pattern between 50BPM & 100BPM.

High or Low heart rate

A heartrate below 50BPM or above 120BPM in EKG version 1 affects the EKG application's ability to check for Atrial fibrillation

- A low heartrate can be as a result of some medications or if electrical signals aren't properly conducted through the heart.
- A heartrate can be high because of AFib, alcohol, stress, infection, nervousness, infection, exercise, or other arrhythmias.

Inconclusive

An inconclusive result means that the ECG application cannot classify the result

View & share your health info

ECG waves, related classifications, and all detected symptoms will be stored in the Health application on your phone. You can also share a PDF with your doctor.

- Launch the Health application.
- Click the "Browse" button, touch the Heart button, and then click on the Electrocardiogram (ECG) button.
- Touch the chart to check your ECG results.
- Touch Export PDF to your doctor.
- Touch the Share icon to print or share the PDF file.

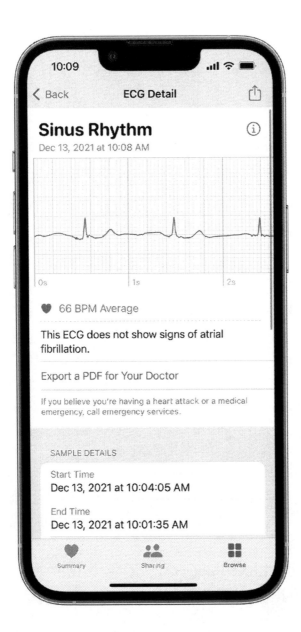

MAPS

The Maps application on the device can be used to explore your surroundings & get directions to locations.

Use Walking Radius to see interesting places around you

The Walking Radius feature shows places of interest close to you.

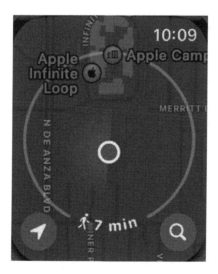

- Launch the Maps application.

The map shows a circle of places that you can go to within minutes.
- Roll the Digital Crown to adjust the radius.

Search the map

- Launch the Map application .
- Touch the Search icon , touch the <u>Search</u> button, and then click on the Dictate button to dictate or the Scribble button to type what you want

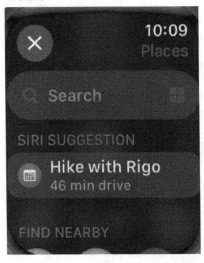

Find a service close to you

- Launch the Maps application.
- Click on the Search button 🔍, touch the Search Locations icon ⊕, and then click on one of the categories like Restaurants.
- Roll the Digital Crown to navigate through the results and view their locations on the map.
- Touch one of the results, and then roll the Digital Crown to see info about it.
- Click the Back button ◁ to go back to the list of results.

View recent locations

- Launch the Maps application

- Click on the Search button 🔍, scroll down, and then touch one of the locations displayed in the Recents section.

Pan & zoom

- Pan the map by dragging with one of your fingers.
- Zoom in or out: Roll the Digital Crown.
  You can also tap the map two times to get close to where you tapped.
- Return to your location: Touch the Location button ➤.

Get Directions

- Launch the Maps application.
- Touch the Search icon 🔍, and then roll the Digital Crown to navigate to Favourites, Recent, Guides, etc.
- Touch one of the entries, touch a destination, and then touch the button in the upper right to select cycling, transit, walking & driving directions.

HEART RATE

Your heart rate is a great way to check your body's health.

Check your heartrate

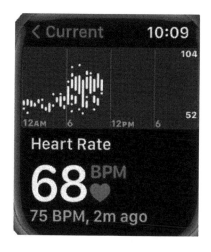

Launch the Heart Rate application to see your heartrate.

The device will continue to measure your heart rate as long as you are putting it on.

View your heartrate data graph

- Launch the Health application on your phone.
- Click the <u>Browse</u> button, touch the <u>Heart</u> button, then touch one of the entries
  You can see your heartrate by the last hour, day, week, month, or year.

Or, launch the Heartrate application on your watch, and roll the Digital Crown to Walking Average, Rest Rate, or Range to see your heart rate for the day.

MINDFULNESS

The Mindfulness application ✱ recommends taking a few minutes to concentrate, & connect as you breathe every day.

Begin a Reflect or Breathe Session

Launch the Mindfulness application, and then carry out any of the below:

- Reflect: Touch the <u>Reflect</u> button, read the topic, focus, and then touch the <u>Begin</u> button.

- Breathe: Touch the Breath button, breathe in slowly as the animation increases, and then breath out as it decreases.

To end the session, swipe right, and then click on the End button.

Set the session duration

- Launch the Mindfulness application.
- Touch the More Options icon, click on the Duration button, and select a duration

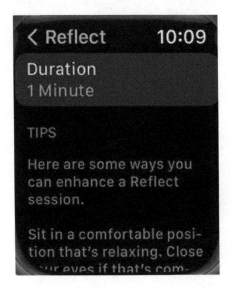

Change the mindfulness settings

Enter your watch's Settings application, click on the Mindfulness button, and then do any of the below:

- Create mindfulness reminder: In the Reminders segment, enable or disable Start of Day & End of Day, click on the Add Reminder button to create more reminders.
- Receive or stop a weekly summary: Enable or disable the Weekly Summary.
- Silent reminder: Enable Mute for today.
- Adjust the breath level: Click on the Breathe Rate button to adjust the number of breaths per minute.
- Select haptics settings: Click on the Haptics button, and then select any of the available options.
- Receive New Meditation: Enable the Add New Meditation to Watch option to download new meditations when your device is charging. Your finished meditations will be automatically erased.

Or, launch the Watch application on your phone, click on the My Watch button, click on the Mindfulness button, and then change any of the settings.

Listen to guided Meditations

If you're subscribed to Apple Fitness+, you can listen to Manual Meditation with your device when it is connected to headphones.

- Launch the Mindfulness application.
- Click on Fitness + Audio Meditation.
- Scroll to view all the Meditations.
  At the bottom of each episode, you'll see the duration, trainer, & theme of the Meditation.
- Touch the Details button ⓘ to get more information about the Meditation, play it in the Music application, and more.
- Touch one of the Meditations to get started.

As the Meditation starts playing, the time spent and your current heartbeat will appear on your watch's screen.

To pause or end a meditation, swipe right while the meditation is playing, and then click on the End or Pause button. You can start a workout while the Meditation is playing, by touching the Workout button, and choosing one of the workouts.

View Meditations you've completed

After completing most or all of a Meditation, it will appear in My Library on your watch.

- Launch the Mindfulness application.
- Click on the Fitness + Audio Meditation button.
- Scroll down, and then click on Library to see the Meditations you have played.
- Touch the Details button ⓘ to get more information about a meditation, play it in the Music application, and more.
- Touch a meditation to replay it.

MEMOJI

You can create your own Memoji with the Memoji application.

Create a Memoji

- Launch the Memoji application.
- If this is the first time you are opening the Memoji application, simply touch the Get Started button.
  If you have created a Memoji before, scroll up and then click the Add button ⊕ to add another Memoji.

- Click on each of the features and roll the Digital Crown to select the option you want for the Memoji.
- Touch the Done button ✓ to add the Memoji to your collections.

Click on the Add button ⊕ to create another Memoji.

Create a Memoji watch face, edit Memoji, etc.

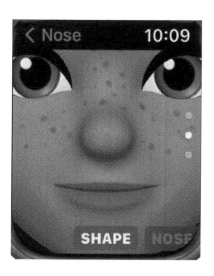

Launch the Memoji application, touch one of the Memoji, and select any of the options:

- Edit a Memoji: Click on features like eye and headbands, and roll Digital Crown to pick variations.
- Create a Memoji watch face: Scroll down, and click on the <u>Create Watch Face</u> button.
  Go back to your watch face and swipe left to view the Memoji watch face.
- Duplicate a Memoji: Scroll down, and then click on the <u>Duplicate</u> button.
- Delete a Memoji: Scroll down, and then click on the <u>Delete</u> button.

MUSIC

You can add music to your watch and listen to it any time you like, even when your phone is not with you.

Add music using your iPhone

- Launch the Watch application on your phone.
- Touch the My Watch button, and then click on the Music button.
- Touch the Add Music button under Playlist & Album.
- Navigate to the playlists & albums you would like to synchronize to your watch, and then touch the Add icon ⊕ to the queue.

The music will be added to your watch when it's placed close to your iPhone.

Add music with your watch

If you are subscribed to Apple Music, you can add songs with your watch.

- Launch the Music application.
- On the Listen Now display, go to the song you would like to add.
Or, from the Listen Now display, click on the Back button , click on the Search button, and then search for the song you would like to add.
- Click on one of the albums or playlists, click the More Options button , and then touch the Add to Library button.
A message would confirm that the music has been added.
- To download the music to your device, touch the More button and then click on the Download button.

Add a workout playlist

Add a playlist that will automatically start playing when you begin a workout in the Workout application.

- Launch the Watch application on your phone.

- Click on the My Watch button, and then click on the Workout button.
- Touch the Workout Playlists button, and select one of the playlists.

The playlist would be added to My Watch> Music in the Watch application on your phone.

Remove music using your phone

- Launch the Watch application on your Phone.
- Click on the My Watch button, click on the Music button, and do any of the below:
    - For the songs you have added: Touch the Edit button and then touch the Delete button beside the items you would like to erase.
    - For automatically added songs: Disable Recent Music or other automatically added songs.

The songs you delete from your watch will remain on your phone.

Remove music using your watch

If you are subscribed to Apple Music, you can delete songs from your watch.

- Launch the Music application on your watch.
- From the Listen Now display, click on the Back button, scroll down, touch the <u>Downloaded</u> button, and then touch Albums or Playlist.
- Touch any of the albums or playlists, click the More Options button, and then touch the <u>Remove</u> button.
- Select any of the options:
  - ✓ Delete from Library
  - ✓ Remove Downloads

Note: You can also delete a song from your library. Swipe a song to the left, touch the More Options button, click on the <u>Delete from Library</u> button, and then touch the Delete button.

Playing songs

After connecting your watch to your headphones or Bluetooth speakers, launch the Music application, and then do any of the below:

- Play songs on your device: Roll the Digital Crown to navigate through the Listen Now display, and then touch one of the albums, playlists, or categories.
- Play songs from your Music Library: From the Listen Now display, touch the Back button, click on the <u>Library</u> button, touch one of the categories like Downloaded, Albums, Playlists, or one of the recently added items, and then select music.
- Request songs from Apple Music (you need to subscribe to Apple Music): Raise your hand, then request a song, album, artist, a part of the lyrics, or genre.

- Search the Apple Music library: Click on the Search button, type a song, artist, or album, and then touch the Search button. Touch one of the results to play it.

Listen to Apple Music radio

If you want to listen to Apple Music radio, ensure your watch is close to your phone or connected to a WiFi or mobile network.

- Launch the Music application.
- From the Listen Now display, touch the Back button , click on the Radio button, and then touch Apple Music Country, Apple Music Hit, or Apple Music 1.

STOPWATCH APP

Use the Stopwatch application to easily time events.

Launch & select a stopwatch

- Enter the Stopwatch application.
- Roll the Digital Crown to select another format. You can pick Digital, Hybrid, or Analog.

Begin, end, and reset the stopwatch

Launch the Stopwatch application, roll the Digital Crown to pick one of the formats, and then do any of the below:

- Start: Touch the Start button .
- Touch the Lap button to record a lap.
- Touch the Stop button to record the final time.
- After the stopwatch stops, touch the Reset button to reset the stopwatch.

The timing will continue even if you return to the watch face or launch another application.

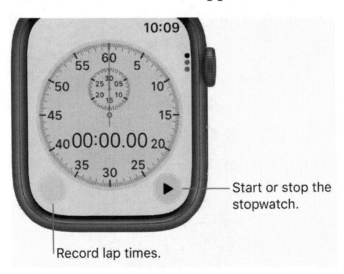

Start or stop the stopwatch.

Record lap times.

TIMER APP

You can use the Timer application to keep track of time.

Set a quick Timer

- Launch the Timers application.
- To start the timer, touch one of the durations or touch one of the timers you have recently used in the Recents section. Touch the Add button ⊕ to setup a custom timer.

Stop or pause a timer

- While the timer is running in the Timers application.
- Touch the Pause button ▌▌ to pause the timer, click on the Play button ▶ to continue, or click on the Cancel button ✕ to end.

Create a custom timer

- Launch the Timers application, and then touch the Add button ⊕.
- Touch seconds, minutes, or hours; roll the Digital Crown to make adjustments

- Click on the <u>Start</u> button.

Create multiple timers

- Launch the Timers application.
- Create & begin the timer
- Touch the Add button ⊕ to go back to the main screen, then create and begin another timer.

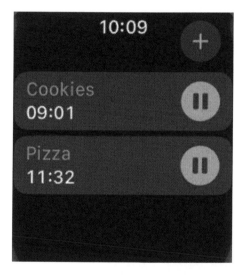

Touch the Back button ◄ to show all your running timers on the Main screen. Touch the Pause button ❚❚ to pause a timer, and touch the Continue button ▶ to continue.

To remove a timer from the Timer screen, simply swipe left on the timer, and then touch the X button.

NOISE

The Noise application can measure the noise level around you through your watch's microphone and exposure duration. When your device notices that the decibel level has reached the level where hearing can be affected, it can inform you by tapping your wrist.

Configure the Noise application

- Launch the Noise application.
- Touch the Enable button to activate monitoring.

- To get a measurement of the noise level around you from now on, just enter the Noise application.

Receive noise alerts

- Enter your watch's Settings application.
- Touch Noise> Noise Notification, and select one of the settings.

Or, launch the Watch application on your phone, click on the <u>My Watch</u> button, then navigate to Noise> Noise Threshold.

Disable noise measuring

- Enter your watch's Settings application.
- Touch Noise> Environmental Sounds Measurement, and then disable Measure Sound.

Or, launch the Watch application on your phone, click on the <u>My Watch</u> button, click on Noise, and then disable Environmental Sounds Measurement.

See the details about noise notifications

You can receive messages from your watch on your phone when the sound around you gets to a level that may affect your hearing.

Adhere to the guidelines below to see the details of a notification:

- Launch the Health application on your phone, and click on the <u>Summary</u> button.
- Touch the notification at the upper part of your display, and then click on the <u>Show More Details</u> button.

SLEEP APP

You can create sleep schedules to help you achieve your sleep goals on your watch. Put on your watch to bed, and your device will help monitor your sleep. After waking up, enter the Sleep application to get more info about your sleep and view your sleep trends for the last fourteen days.

You can set up more than one sleep schedule - for instance, one for weekdays & one for weekends. You can setup the following for each schedule:

- Sleep goals (how long you want to sleep)
- When you want to go to bed & wakeup
- An alarm to wake you

- When to enable Sleep Focus mode, which reduces distractions before you sleep
- Sleep monitoring, which makes use of your movements to detect sleep when you put on your watch to bed and the Sleep Focus is enabled.

Learn more: To disable Sleep Focus, long-press the Digital Crown to unlock your device, press your watch's side button to enter the Controls Centre, and then touch the Sleep mode button 🛏.

Setup Sleep on your device

- Launch the Sleep application.
- Adhere to the directives on your display.

Or, launch the Health application on your phone, touch the Browse button, touch the Sleep button, and then click on Get Started under Setup Sleep.

Modify or deactivate your next wakeup alarm

- Launch the Sleep application.

- Touch the Wakeup Alarm button 🔔.

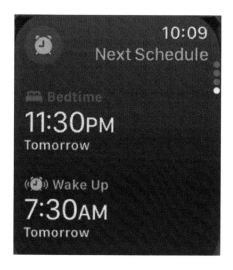

- To create a new wakeup time, click on the wakeup time, roll the Digital Crown to select a new wakeup time, and then touch the Done button ✓.
  If you do not want your device to wake you up in the morning, disable Alarm.

Or, launch the Health application on your phone, click on the Browse button, touch the Sleep button, and then touch the Edit button in the Your Schedule section to make adjustments to your schedule.

This change only applies to your next wake-up alarm, after which your normal routine returns.

Modify or add sleep schedules

- Launch the Sleep application.
- Touch the Wakeup Alarm button .
- Roll the Digital Crown to navigate to Full Schedule, and then do any of the below:
  - Change a schedule: Click on the current one.
  - Add a sleep schedule: Click on the Add Schedules button.
  - Adjust your sleep goals: Touch the Sleep Goal button, and then choose how long you want to sleep.
  - Change wind-down time: Click on the Wind Down button, and then choose how long you want Sleep Focus mode to be activated before your bed time.
- Do any of the below:
  - Set your schedule days: Touch your schedule, then click on Active On, select the days, and then click on the Back button .
  - Change the wake & sleep time: Touch your schedule, click on Wakeup or Bedtime, roll the Digital Crown to choose a new time, and then click on the Done button .

- Set the alarm options: Touch your schedule, then disable or enable Alarm, and touch Sounds & Haptic to pick an alarm sound.
- Delete or cancel a sleep schedule: Touch your schedule, and then click on the <u>Delete Schedule</u> button in the lower part of your display, to delete a schedule, or click the Cancel button ⊗ to stop creating a schedule.

Change sleep options

- Enter your watch's Settings application.
- Click on the <u>Sleep</u> button, and then change any of the following settings:
  - Activate at Wind Down: As a rule, Sleep Focus starts at the wind-down time you set in the Sleep application. If you want to manually control Sleep Focus in the Controls Centre, disable this option.
  - Sleep Screen: Your watch's screen and iPhone's Lock Screen are simplified to lessen distractions.
  - Show Time: Display the time & date on your phone & watch when Sleep Focus mode is activated.

- Enable or disable Charging Reminders & Sleep Tracking.
When sleep Tracking is activated, your device will monitor your sleep and add sleep info to the Health application on your phone.

Check your sleep history

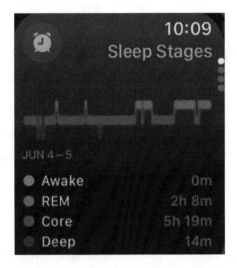

Launch the Sleep application to check how much sleep you had last night and your average *sleep* over the past 14 days.

To view your sleep history on your phone, enter the Health application on your phone, touch the Browse button, and then click on the Sleep button.

Check your sleep breathing rate

Your device can help you monitor your respiratory rate while you sleep, which can give you more information about your well-being. After putting on your watch to bed, adhere to the directions below:

- Launch the Health application on your phone, click on the <u>Browse</u> button, and then click on the <u>Respiratory</u> button.
- Click on the <u>Respiratory Rate</u> button, and then click on Show More Respiratory Data.

Deactivate breathing rate measurements

- Enter your watch's Settings application
- Touch Privacy and Security> Health
- Click on the <u>Respiratory Rate</u> button, and then disable Respiratory Rate.

Or, launch the Watch application on your phone, click on the <u>My Watch</u> button, click on Privacy, and then disable Respiratory Rate.

WALKIE-TALKIE

Walkie-Talkie is an interesting and easy way to keep in touch with other Apple Watch users. Walkie-Talkie requires that the two individuals participating connect to an iPhone, WiFi, or cellular via Bluetooth.

Invite your friend to use Walkie-Talkie

- Launch the Walkie-Talkie application.
- Scroll to look for a contact in the list, and then touch a name to send an invitation.

After your invitation has been accepted by the contact, you can begin a Walkie-Talkie conversation when the two of you are available.

To add another contact, click on the Add Friend button on the Walkie-Talkie display, and then select one of the contacts.

Have a conversation

- Launch the Walkie-Talkie application.
- Touch the name of your friend.
- Long-press the Talk button, then start talking.
  If your friend chooses to make themselves available, the Walkie-Talkie application will open

on their watch and they will be able to hear what you're saying.

Roll the Digital Crown to change the volume level as you speak.

Talk with a tap

If you're having trouble long-pressing the Talk button, you can make use of a single tap to talk.

- Enter your watch's Settings application.
- Click on the <u>Accessibility</u> button, and then enable <u>Tap to Talk</u> in the Walkie-Talkie section.

Or, launch the Watch application, click on the <u>My Watch</u> button, click on Accessibility, and then activate Tap to Talk in the Walkie-Talkie section.

When you're done, touch once to speak, and then touch one more time when you are done speaking.

Remove contacts

Swipe left on a contact in the Walkie-Talkie application, then click on the **X** button.

Make yourself unavailable

- Press your watch's side button to reveal the Controls Centre.
- Scroll, and then click on the Walkie-Talkie button.

You can also enter the Walkie-Talkie application, scroll to the top, and then disable Walkie-Talkie.

VOICE MEMOS

You can use the Voice Memos application to record notes.

Record a voice memo

- Launch the Voice Memos application.
- Touch the Record button ●.
- Touch the End button ● when you want to stop recording.

Play a voice memo

- Launch the Voice Memos application.
- Touch any of the recordings in the Voice Memos screen, and then click on the Play button ▶ to play it.
- Touch the Skip Back button ⊚ or the Skip Ahead button ⊚ to skip back or skip ahead
- To delete a record, or change its name, click on the More Options button ⊚ and then click on the Delete button or the Edit Name button.

APPLE PAY

Apple Pay provides a reliable, easy, & private way to pay for items using your watch

Add a card to your watch

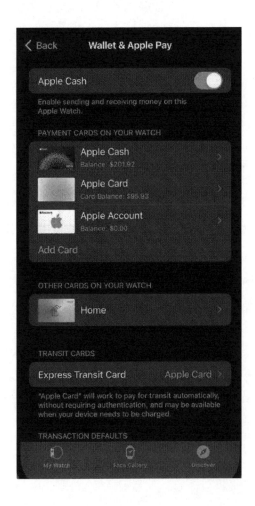

- Launch the Watch application on your phone.
- Touch the <u>My Watch</u> button, and then click on the <u>Wallet and Apple Pay</u> button.
- If you have a card on another Apple device or you've recently removed a card, touch the Add button beside the card you want to add and enter the CVV of the card.
- For other cards, click on the <u>Add Card</u> button and then adhere to the directions on your display.

Your card provider might ask for more steps to verify your ID.

Add cards on your watch

- Launch the Wallet application on your watch
- Click on the More Options button , and then click on the <u>Add Card</u> button
- Choose the type of card, and then adhere to the directives on your display.

Select a default card

- Launch the Wallet application
- Click on the More Options button, click on the Default Card button, and then pick any of the cards.

Or, launch the Watch application on your phone, click on the My Watch button, tap on Wallet and Apple Pay, click on the Default Card, and then pick one of the cards.

Rearrange payment cards

Launch the Wallet application, long-press a card, and then move the card to another position by dragging it there.

Remove a card

- Launch the Wallet application.
- Touch the card to select it.
- Scroll, and then touch the Remove button.

Or, launch the Watch application on your phone, click on the My Watch button, tap on Wallet and

Apple Pay, touch one of the cards, and then click on the Remove Card button.

Find a card's Device Account number

When making a payment with your watch, the card's Device Account Number is sent to the retailer. To look for the last 4 digits of this number, adhere to the guidelines below:

- Launch the Wallet application.
- Touch a card to select it, and then touch Card Detail.

Or, launch the Watch application on your phone, click on the My Watch button, tap on Wallet and Apple Pay, and then touch a card.

Edit the transaction information

You can change your in-application transaction info, which includes shipping address, number, e-mail & default card.

- Enter the Watch application on your phone.

- Touch <u>My Watch</u> button, click on <u>Wallet and Apple Pay</u>, and then scroll to see Transactions Default.
- Touch any of the items to change it.

Use your watch to pay for items in a store

- Press the side button twice quickly.
- Scroll down to select a card.
- Place your watch very close to the contactless card reader and ensure your watch's screen is facing the reader.

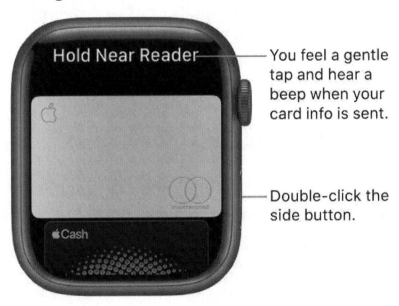

A tap & beep will indicate that the payment info has been sent.

Make purchases within an application

- When buying something in an application on your watch, just select the Apple Pay option when checking out.
- Go through the necessary details, and then click the side button two times quickly to pay with your watch.

WORLD CLOCK APP

You can check the time in different cities around the world on your device.

Add and remove cities from the World Clock app

- Launch the World Clock application.
- Click on the List button , then click the Add button .
- Type the city's name
- Touch the city's name to add it to the World Clock.

To delete a city from the list, swipe left on the city's name in the cities list, then touch the **X** button.

See the time in other cities

- Launch the World Clock application.

- Click on the List button ●, then roll the Digital Crown to surf through the cities list.
- To learn more about any of the cities, including sunrise and sunset times, simply touch the city in the cities list.
- When you are done, touch the Back button ● to go back to the cities list.

Edit cities abbreviations

- Launch the Watch application on your iPhone.
- Click on the <u>My Watch</u> button, then head over to Clock> City Abbreviation.
- Touch any of the cities to edit its abbreviation.

WORKOUT APPLICATION

The Workout application provides tools that can help you manage your personal workout sessions.

Begin a workout

- Launch the Workout application.
- Roll the Digital Crown to scroll to the workout you are looking for.
  Click on the <u>Add Workout</u> button in the lower part of your display to see other workouts.

- When you are ready to begin, click the Start workout.

Pause/resume a workout

Press the Digital Crown and the side button simultaneously to pause a workout. You can also swipe right on the workout screen, and then choose one of the options.

Begin an outdoor push workout

If you are a wheelchair user, you can do an outdoor push workout. Your device will track your pushes and you can choose between running pace and walking pace.

Set your status

Adhere to the directions below to set your wheelchair status:

- Launch the Watch application on your phone

- Touch the <u>My Watch</u> button, click on <u>Health,</u> and then click on the <u>Health Details</u> button.
- Touch the <u>Edit</u> button, click on <u>Wheelchair</u>, and then choose Yes
- Touch the <u>Done</u> button when you are done.

Begin an outdoor push exercise

- Launch the Workout application.
- Roll the Digital Crown to either Outdoor Push Walking Pace or Outdoor Push Running Pace.
- Touch the workout when you are ready to begin.

Listen to music while working out

While working out, swipe left to the Now Playing screen; from there, you can select songs and change the volume of your headphones. To pick a playlist that will automatically start playing when you start a workout, enter the Watch application on your phone, touch the <u>My Watch</u> button, touch the <u>Workout</u> button, click on the <u>Workout Playlists</u> button, and then pick any of the playlists.

Change workout views while working out

Begin a workout, then roll the Digital Crown to cycle through the different formats.

Customize workouts views

- Launch the Workout application.
- Roll the Digital Crow to the workout you're looking for.
- Click on the More Options button, and then click on the Preferences button
- Click on [Name of Workout] Workout Views

- Go through the different views, and then touch the Include button beside the metrics you like

Use gym equipment with your watch

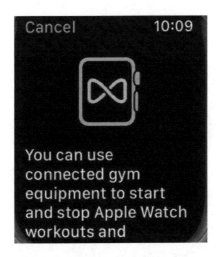

Your device can connect & synchronize information with compatible gym equipment, like indoor bikes, ellipticals, treadmills, etc., and give you more precise info about your workouts.

- Make sure the gym device is compatible – you will see "Connect to Apple Watch" on the device.
- Ensure your watch can detect gym equipment – enter your watch's Settings application, click on the Workout button, and then activate the Detect Gym Equipment setting.

- Bring your watch very close to the contactless reader on the gym equipment, and ensure your watch's screen is facing the reader.
You will feel a soft tap and hear a beep when your watch connects to the gym equipment
- Press the <u>Start</u> button on the gym equipment to start a workout. Press the <u>Stop</u> button when you want to end the workout session.

If the Detect Gym Equipment feature is disabled in the Setting application, enter the Workout application, then take your watch very close to the gym equipment's contactless reader, and ensure your watch's screen is facing the reader.

Check your progress while working out

Raise your hand to see your workout statistics, which include your goal ring, time spent, average speed, covered distance, consumed calories & heartrate. Roll the Digital Crown to see more Workout views. You can get voice feedbacks for essential alerts. To enable or disable the Voice Feedback feature, enter your watch's Settings application, click on the <u>Workouts</u> button, and then touch Voice Feedbacks

End the workout

After reaching your target, your watch will play a sound and vibrate. If you still want to continue, you can —your watch will continue to collect data till you decide to stop. When you are ready to end the workout:

- Swipe to the Right, and then touch the <u>End</u> button.
- Roll the Digital Crown to view the result summary, then touch the Cancel button ⊗ .

Review your workout history

- Enter the Fitness application on your phone.
- Click on the <u>Show More</u> button beside History, and then touch one of the workouts.

Begin a swimming workout

- Launch the Workout application.
- Roll the Digital Crown to choose pool swim or open water swim.

- When you are done, long-press the Digital Crown to unlock your device, click on the <u>End</u> button, and then click on the <u>End Workout</u> button

To pause or resume your swim, Press the side button & the Digital Crown simultaneously.

Clear water from your watch after swimming

When you begin a swim exercise, your device will automatically lock your display with Water Lock to prevent accidental taps. When you come out of the water, long-press the Digital Crown to open the screen and extract any water from the speaker. You'll hear a sound and might feel a little amount of water on your hand.

- After swimming, press your watch's side button to reveal the Controls Centre, and then touch the Water Lock button 💧.
- Long-press the Digital Crown to unlock your display and remove water from your watch's speaker.

See the summary of a swimming exercise

- Unlock your device and then touch the End button.

The pool swimming exercise automatically keeps track of your sets and your resting time. The summary shows the types of strokes you used and how much distance you covered.

Combine many activities in a single workout

- Launch the Workout application.
- Start with the first exercise, for instance, an Outdoor run.
- When you are ready to begin another activity, just swipe right, touch the End button, touch the New Workout button, and then select an exercise.
- When you're done with all your activities, swipe to the right, click on the End button, and then touch the End Workout button.

- Roll the Digital Crown to get to the summary of the results.
- Scroll down, and then click on the <u>Done</u> button to save the workout.

Change your weight & height

- Launch the Watch application
- Touch the <u>My Watch</u> button, touch Health> Health Detail, and then touch the <u>Edit</u> button.
- Click on Weight or Height, then make the needed adjustments.

Automatically pause cycling & running workouts

- Go to your watch's Settings application.
- Touch the <u>Workout</u> button, touch AutoPause, and then activate AutoPause.

Your device will automatically pause & resume your outdoor cycling & running workouts — for instance, if you stop to drink water.

Enable or disable workout reminders

For swimming, running, walking, & other workouts, your watch detects when you are moving and alerts you to start the Workout application. it will also remind you to end your workout in case you forget. Adhere to the directives below to enable or disable workout reminders.

- Enter your watch's Settings application.
- Touch the <u>Workout</u> button, then change the workout reminder settings.

Conserve power during workouts

- Enter your watch's Settings application.
- Click on Workout, and then enable Low Power Mode.

RESTART, RESET, RESTORE, AND UPDATE

Restart your watch

Restart your watch

- Switch off your device: Press the side button till the sliders show up on your screen, and then slide the Power Off slider to the right end.
- Switch on your device: Press the side button till the Apple icon shows on your display.

Note: You cannot restart your device while it is connected to power.

Force restart your watch

Do this only when you are not able to restart your device.

To force restart your device, long-press the side button & the Digital Crown simultaneously for about 10 seconds, till the Apple icon shows on your screen.

Erase your watch

In some cases, you may have to erase your watch, for example, if you forget your password.

Wipe your Apple Watch and settings

- Enter your watch's Settings application.
- Touch General> Reset, click on Erase All Content & Settings, and then insert your watch's passcode.

If you cannot access the Settings app on your watch because you've forgotten your password, connect your watch to its charger, then long-press the side button till you see the sliders on your screen. Long-press the Digital Crown, and touch the Reset button.

Once the reset is complete and your watch restarts, you'll need to pair your watch with your iPhone again.

Restore your watch from a backup

Your watch automatically backs up to your paired phone, and you can restore it from a saved back up.

Backup & restore your watch

- Backup your watch: When paired with your phone, your watch is backed up continuously to your phone. If you unpair your watch from your phone, a backup is performed.
- Restore your watch from a backup: when pairing your watch with the same phone again, or when pairing a new watch with that same iPhone, you can select Restore from Back Up and choose a saved backup on your phone.

Update your watch software

Check for and install software updates

- Launch the Watch application on your iPhone
- Touch the <u>My Watch</u> button, touch General> Software Updates, then, if there is an update, click on the <u>Download & Install</u> option.

Or, enter your watch's Settings application, and touch General>Software Updates.

BOOK INDEX

A

Activity, 12, 110, 115, 116, 117, 118, 119, 120, 121
Airplane, 54, 55, 56
Alarm, 122, 185, 186, 187
Always On, 27, 32, 99
Apple ID, 10, 11, 63, 78, 79
Apple Pay, 12, 196, 197, 198, 199, 200, 201
Apps Store, 32, 49
Apps Switcher, 42, 44, 86

B

Backup, 217
band, 14, 15, 16, 17, 18, 19
battery, 5, 26, 27, 28, 29, 30, 51

blood oxygen, 2, 27, 126, 127
Blood oxygen, 127
Bluetooth, 6, 28, 36, 54, 55, 84, 104, 134, 172, 190
Bold Text, 12, 67
Bracelet, 15
brightness, 57, 67, 68

C

Calculator, 91
camera, 8, 136
Cellular, 27, 89, 90, 91
charge, 5, 26, 29, 125
clock face, 34, 35
Compass, 137, 140, 141, 142, 143, 144, 145, 146
complications, 33, 106, 108, 110, 113

Control Centre, 26, 27, 28, 52, 53, 62
Cover to Mute, 59
Crash Detection, 99, 100
Cycle Tracking, 130, 131, 132, 133

D

DND, 63, 75
Double-Tap, 1, 21, 22

E

ECG, 147, 148, 149, 150, 153
EKGs, 2
emergency, 27, 92, 94, 95, 96, 97, 100

F

Face Gallery, 106, 107, 108, 114
Fall Detection, 97, 98
flashlight, 51, 56, 57

Focus, 22, 62, 63, 64, 65, 66, 75, 127, 132, 184, 186, 187

G

gym, 208, 209

H

Handoff, 85, 86, 87
Handwashing, 82
heart, 2, 27, 147, 148, 151, 152, 159, 160
Home Screen, 23, 31, 42, 45, 74

I

iOS, 6, 49, 50, 62

L

language, 39, 40, 102, 104
Loop, 17, 18
Low Power Mode, 5, 22, 26, 27, 28, 29, 214

M

Maps, 155, 157, 158
Medical ID, 93, 94
Memoji, 166, 167, 168
Mindfulness, 161, 162, 163, 164, 165
Music, 77, 164, 165, 169, 170, 171, 172, 173, 174

N

Nightstand, 124
Noise, 180, 181
notifications, 5, 27, 72, 73, 74, 75, 78, 130, 182

P

passcode, 11, 36, 37, 38, 79, 83, 216
picture, 101, 134, 135, 136
Ping, 60, 61, 62
power, 24, 26, 28, 214, 215

Precision Finding, 60

R

Remote, 134, 135, 136
restart, 215, 216

S

silent mode, 26, 51, 57, 59, 71, 95, 104
Siri, 51, 96, 102, 103, 104, 105
Sleep, 22, 62, 127, 132, 183, 184, 185, 186, 187, 188
Smart Stacks, 76
Snooze, 123
Stopwatch, 175, 176
storage, 5, 48

T

Taptic Time, 51, 71
Theater Mode, 57, 58, 127
Timers, 177, 178, 179

U

Updates, 49, 218

V

video, 134, 135
Voice Memos, 194, 195

W

Walkie-Talkie, 57, 190, 191, 192, 193
Wallet, 76, 197, 198, 199, 200
watchOS, 10, 12
widgets, 76, 77
WiFi, 6, 12, 27, 54, 55, 58, 83, 88, 97, 174, 190
Workout, 164, 170, 171, 204, 206, 207, 208, 209, 210, 211, 212, 213, 214
World Clock, 202

Made in the USA
Middletown, DE
17 June 2024